This coloring book is great for all coloring fans .This collection of different designs and Patterns is both stimulating and addictive .Demanding and pleasant in equal measure.

This book contains 50 patterns with blank back pages, so you are sure to be able to color with confidence of not ruining your masterpiece due to a bleed through on the page bottom of form

Relax and unwind as you color these dazzling illustrations. Get more value for your money with this amazing adult coloring book.

THIS COLORING BOOK

BELONGS TO :

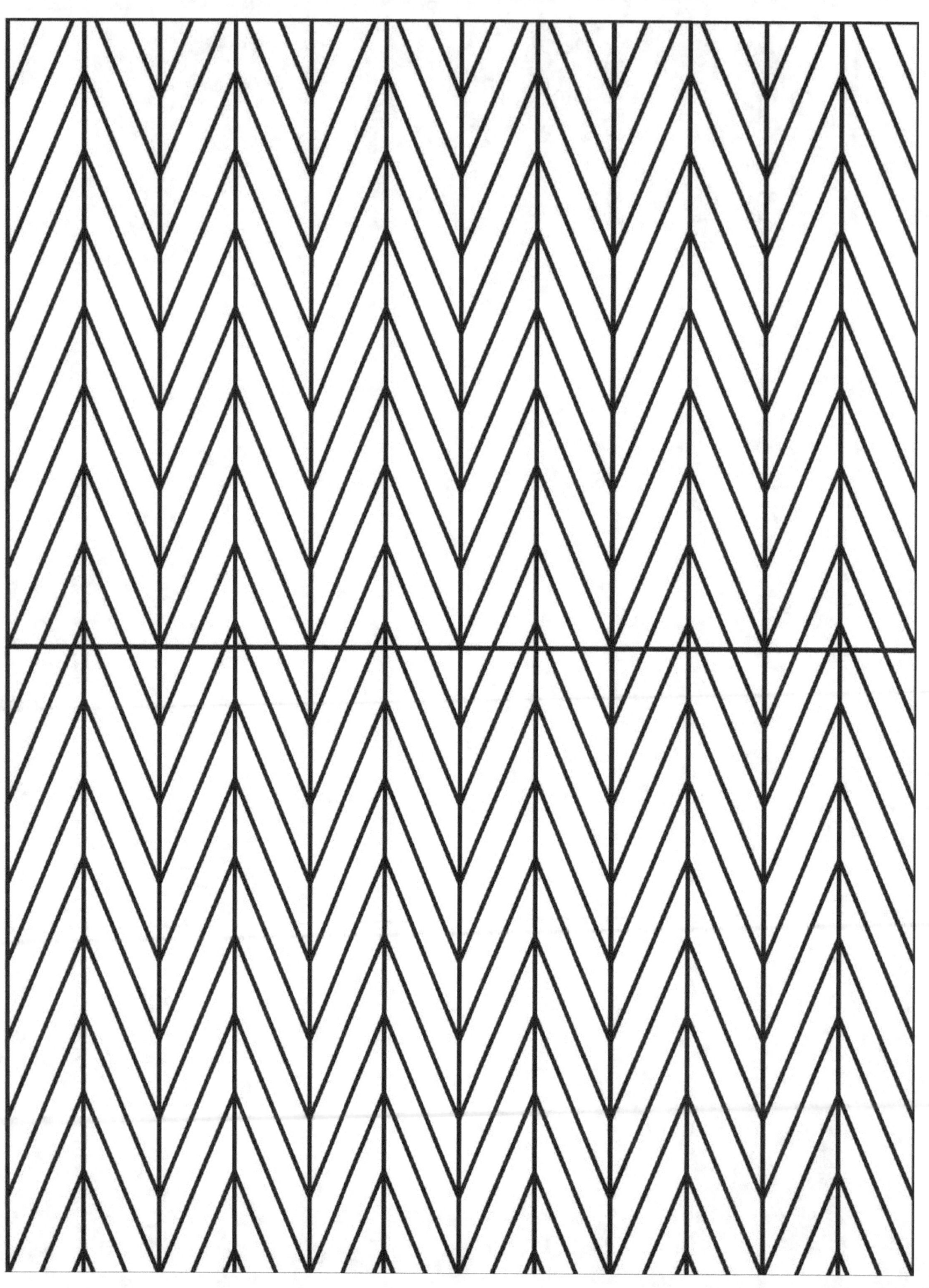

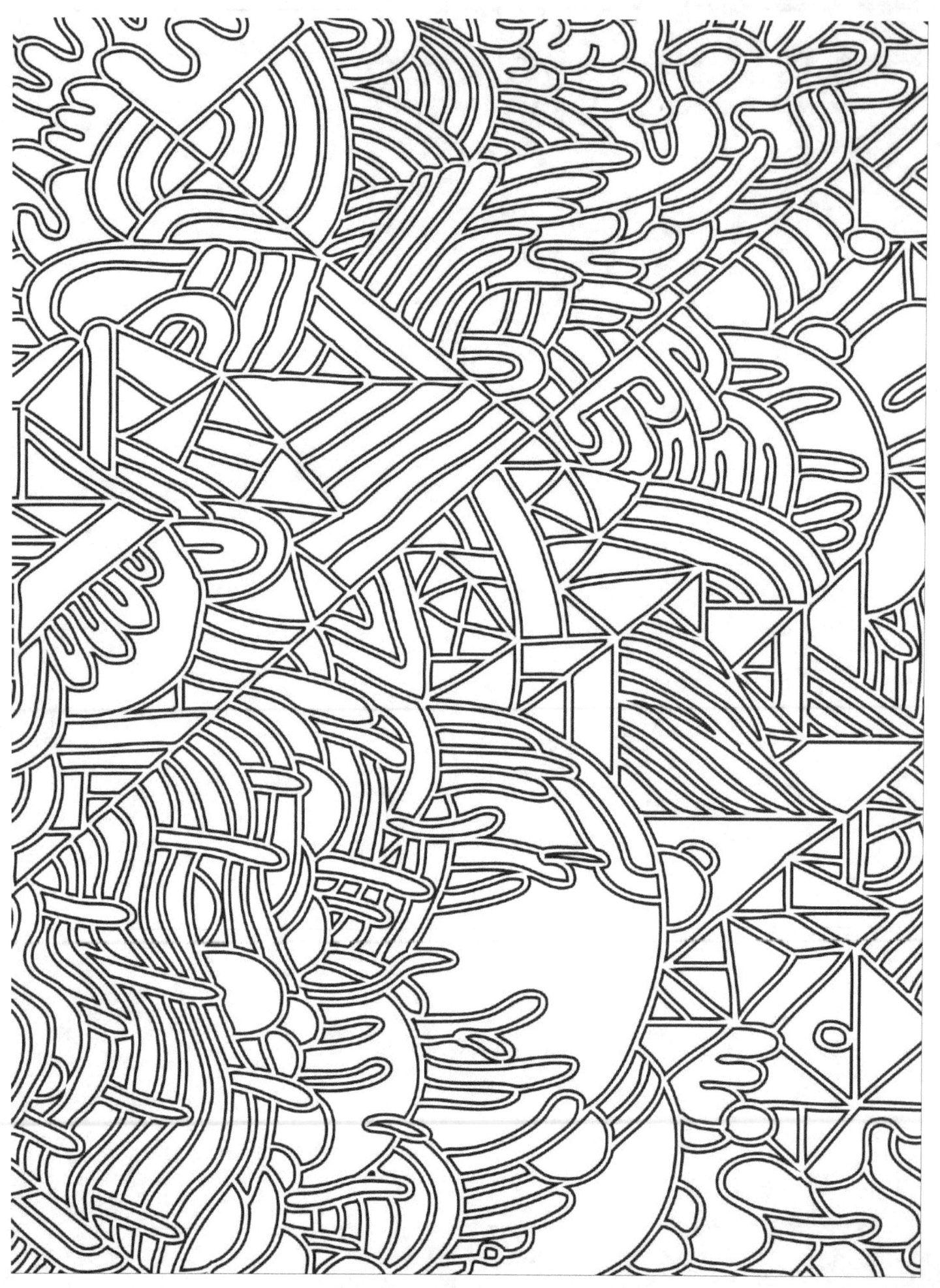

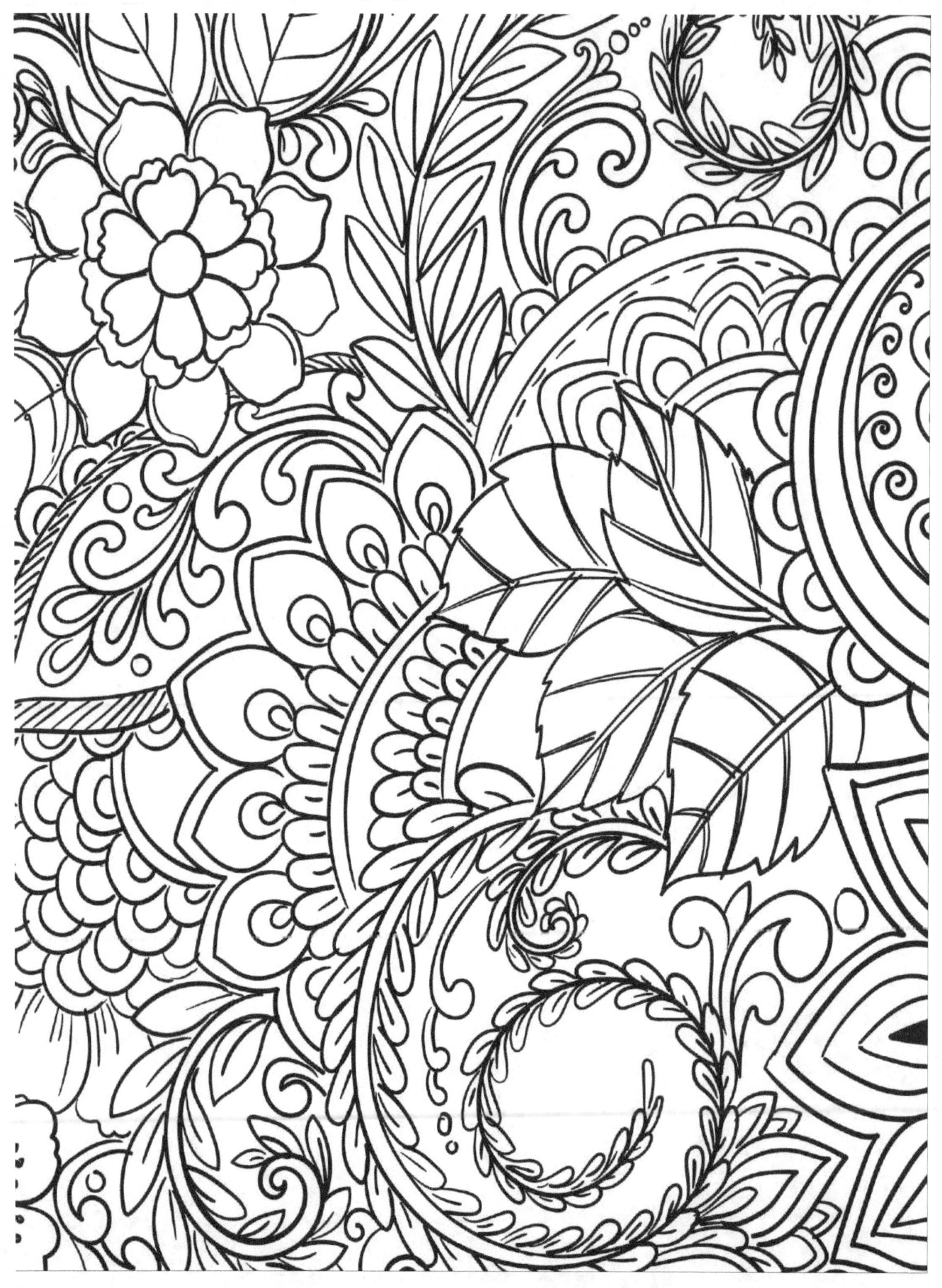

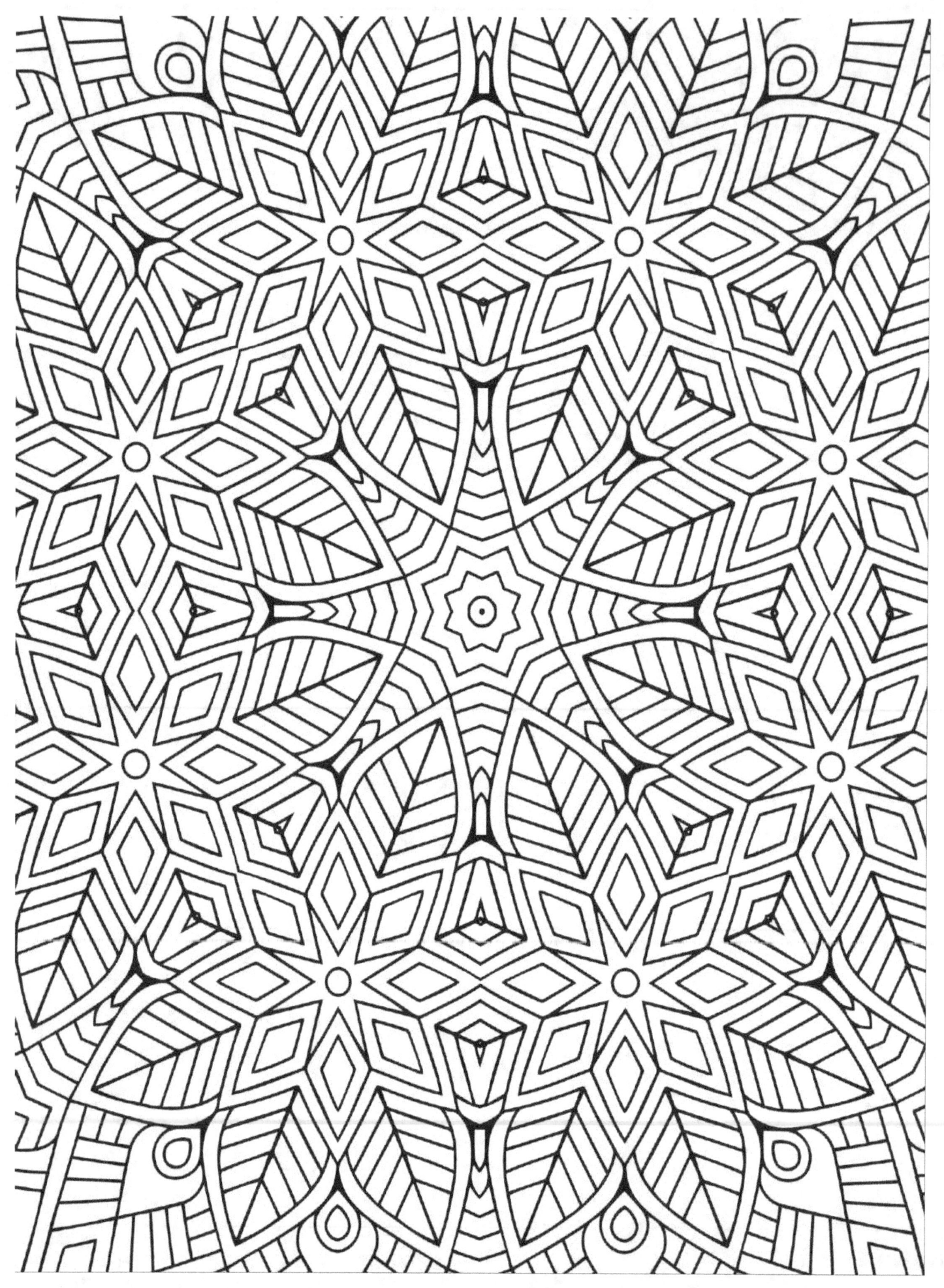

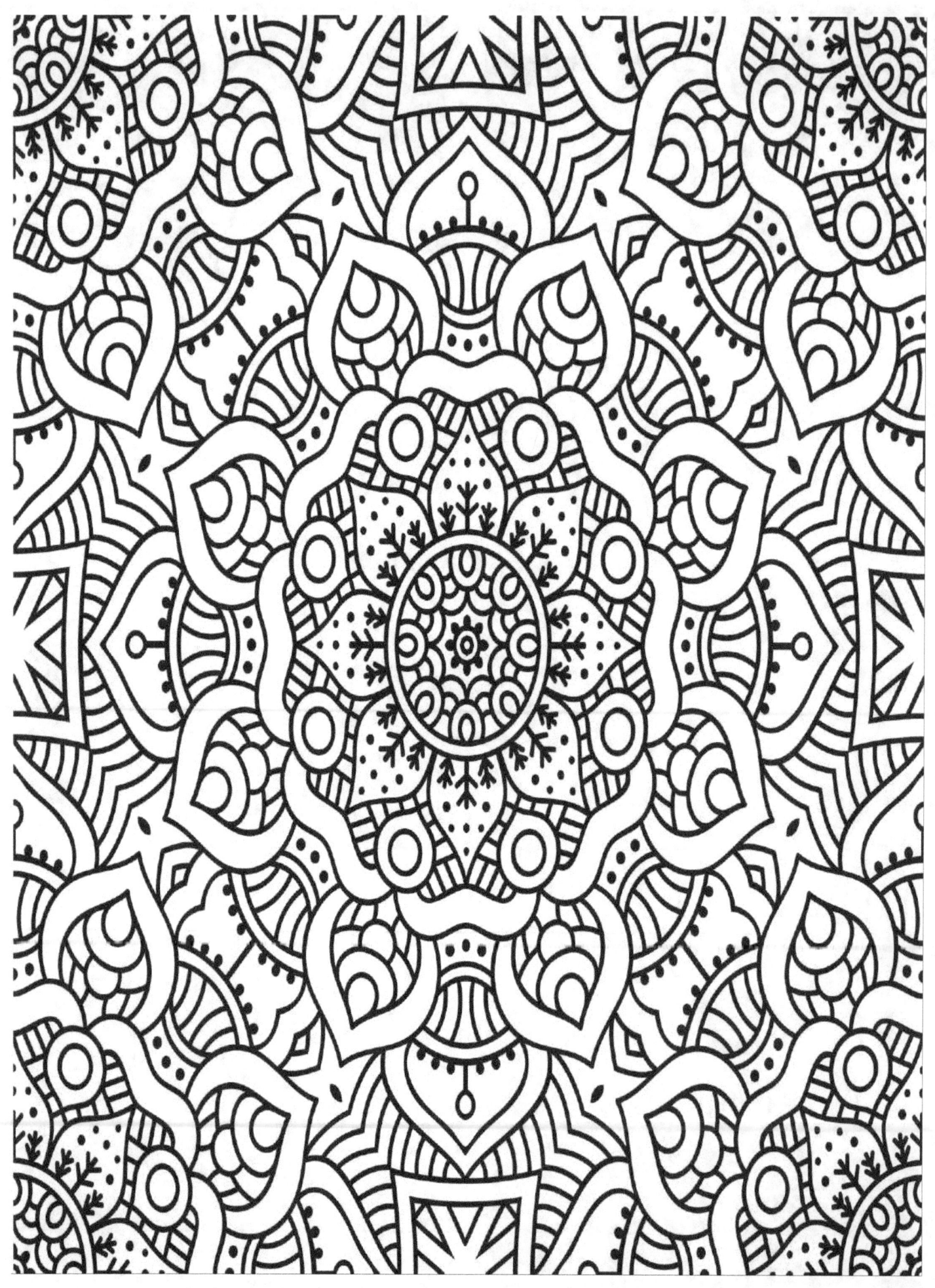

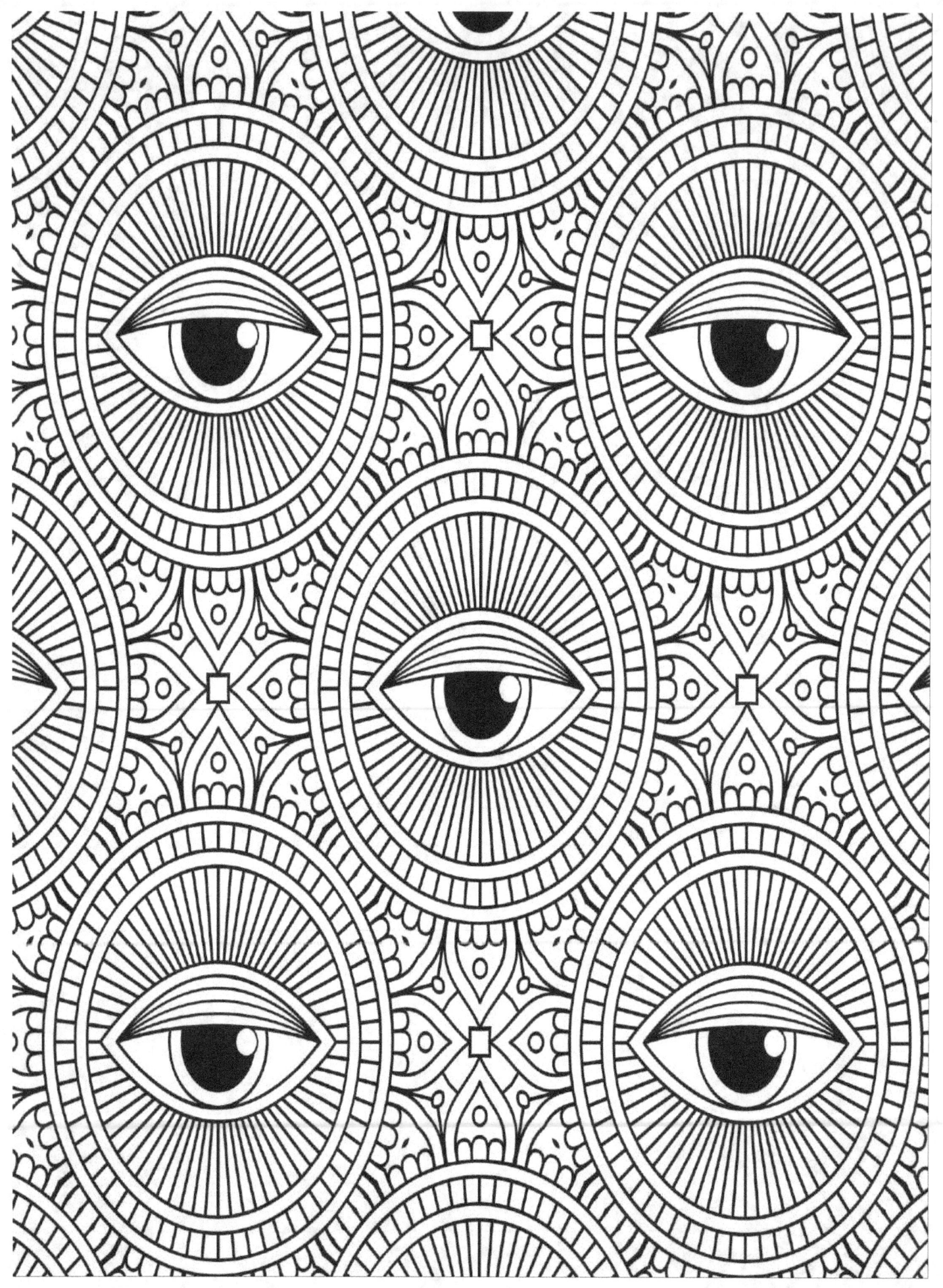

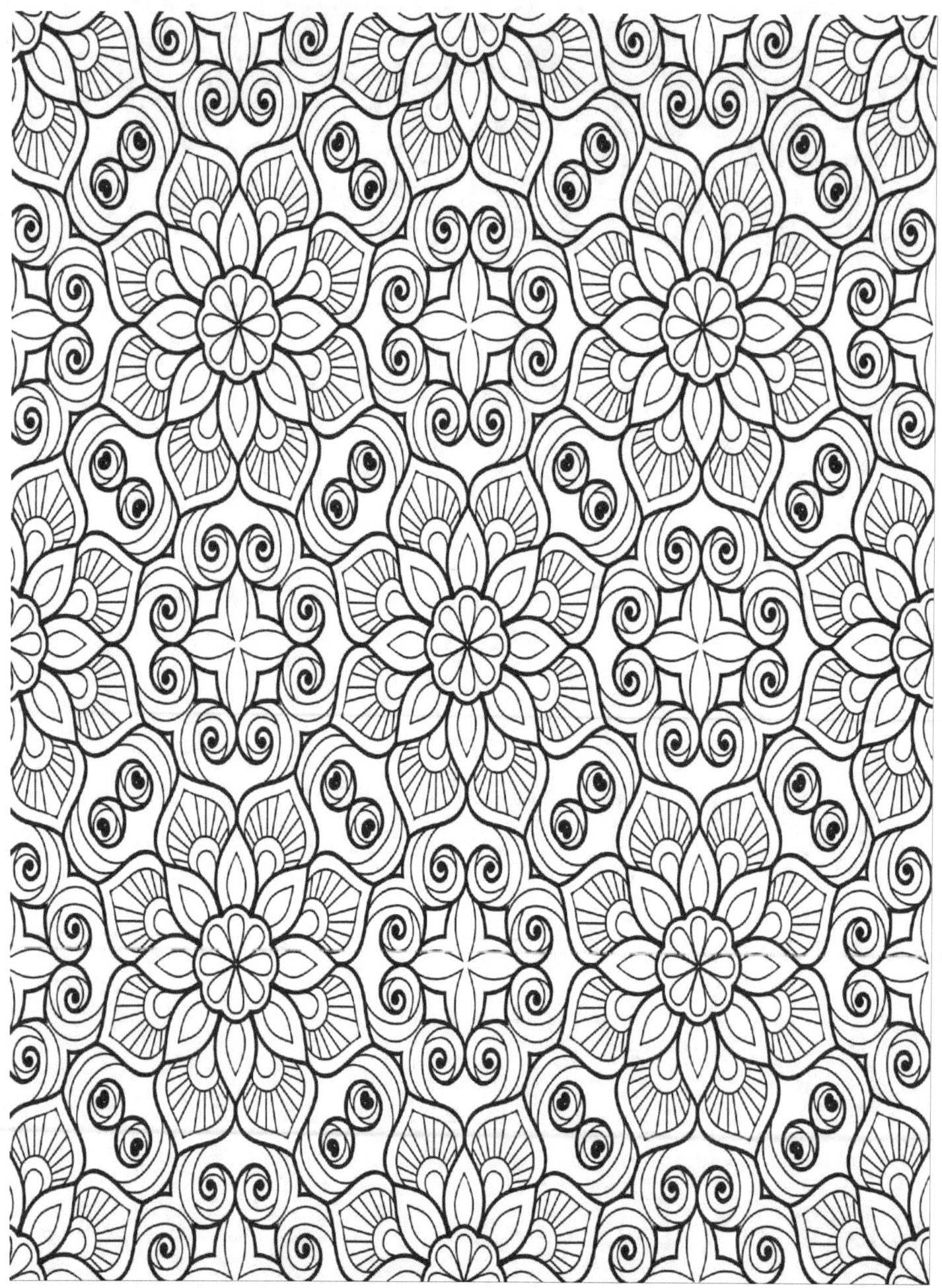

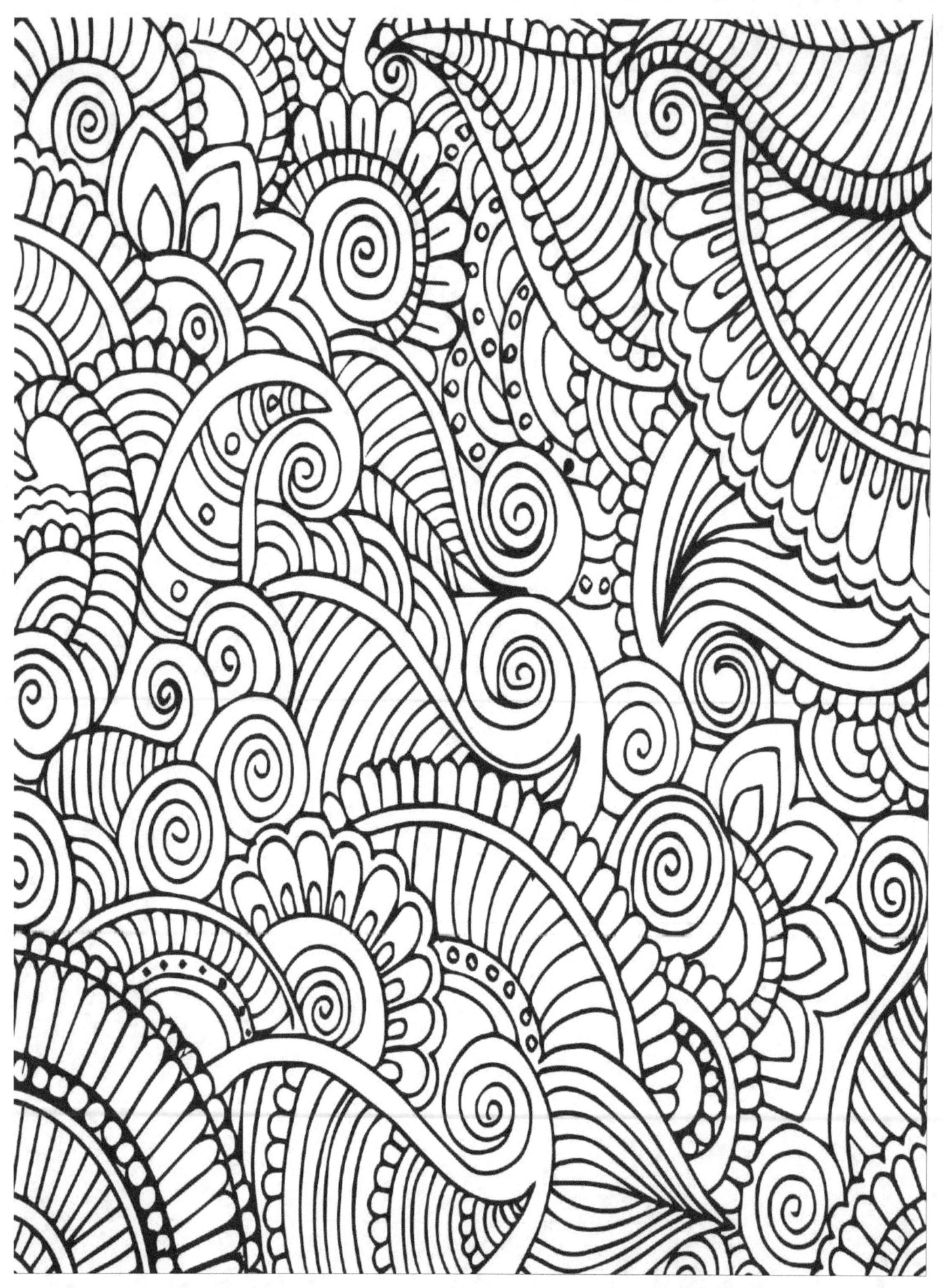

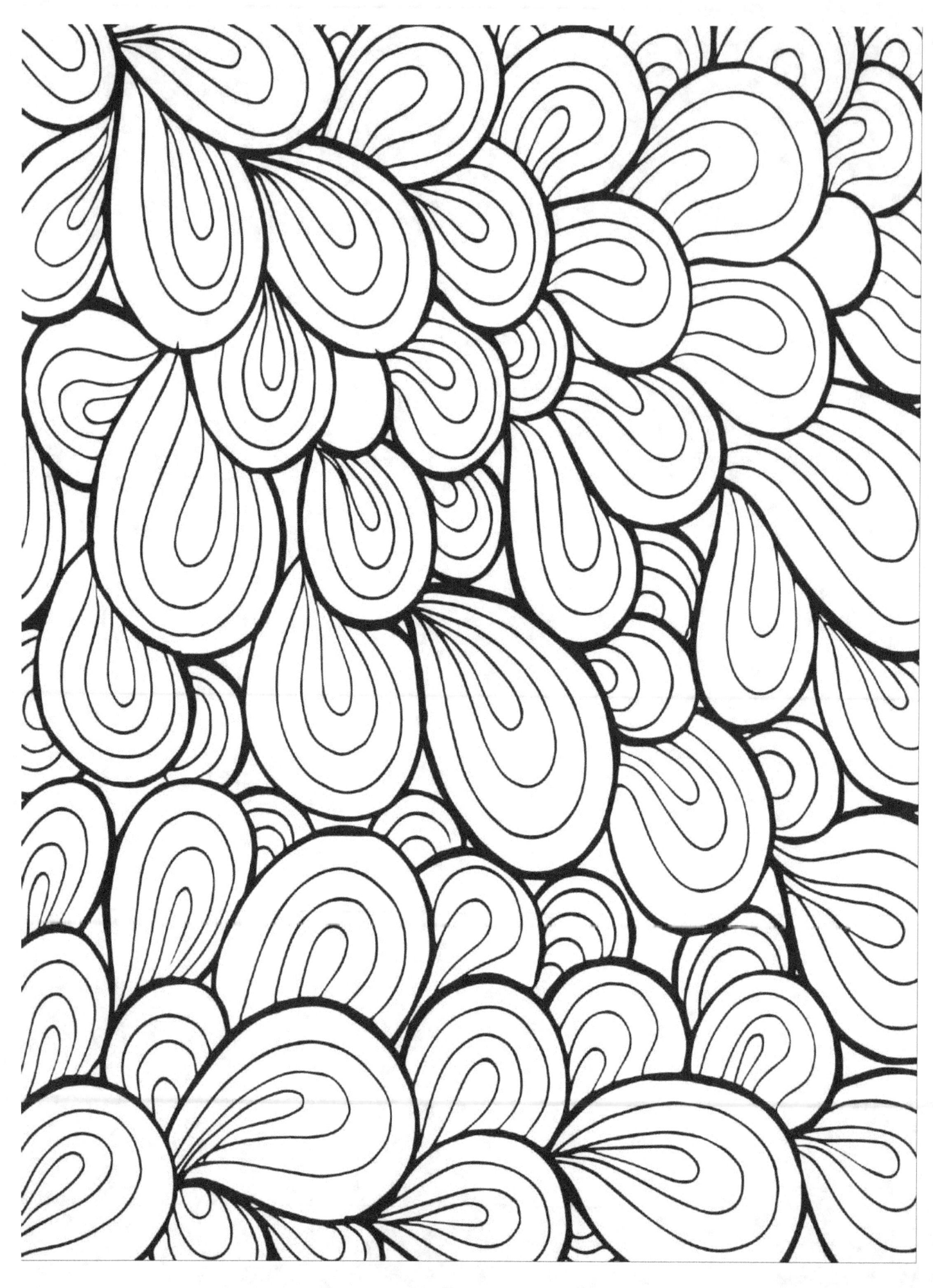

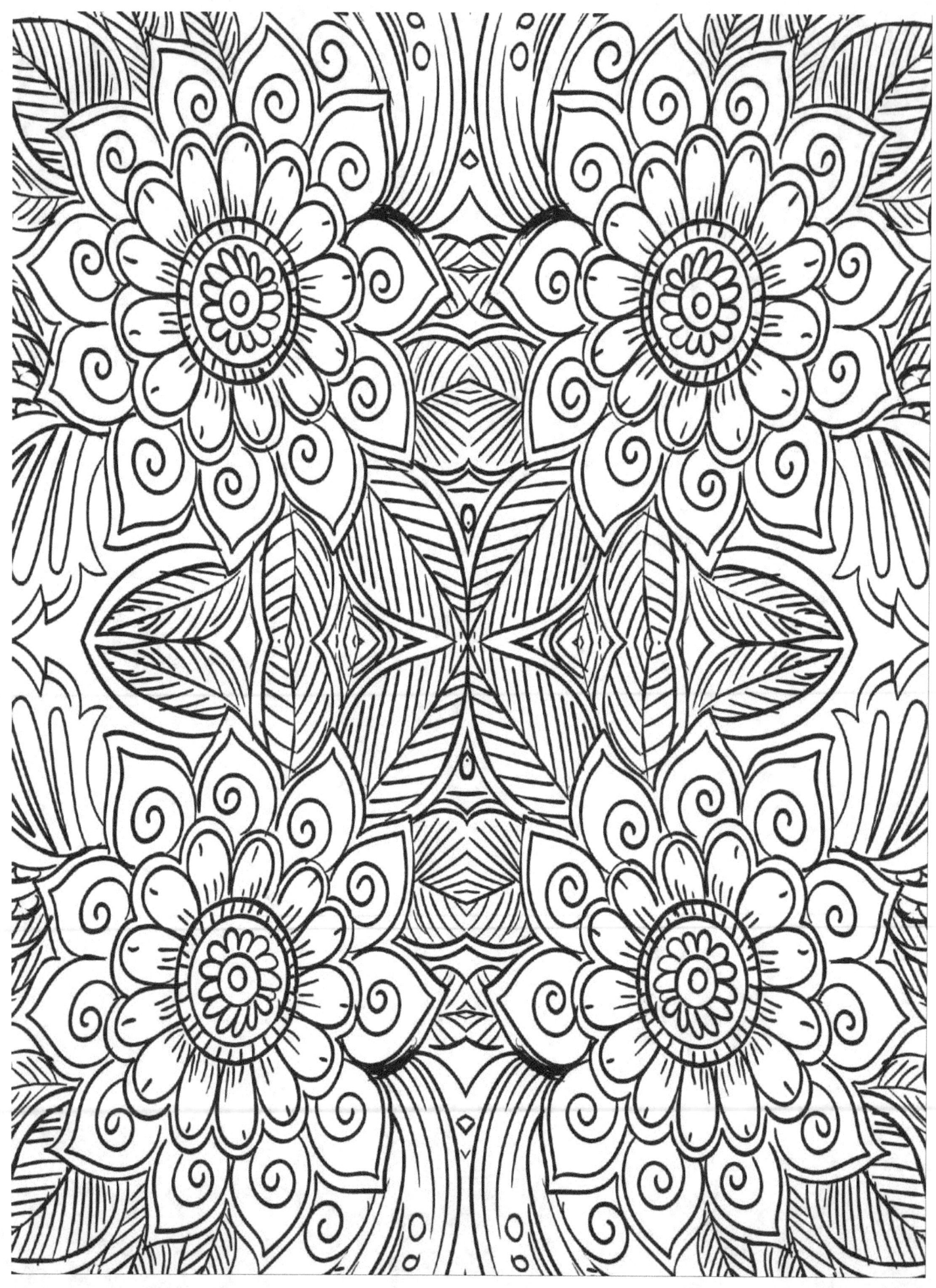

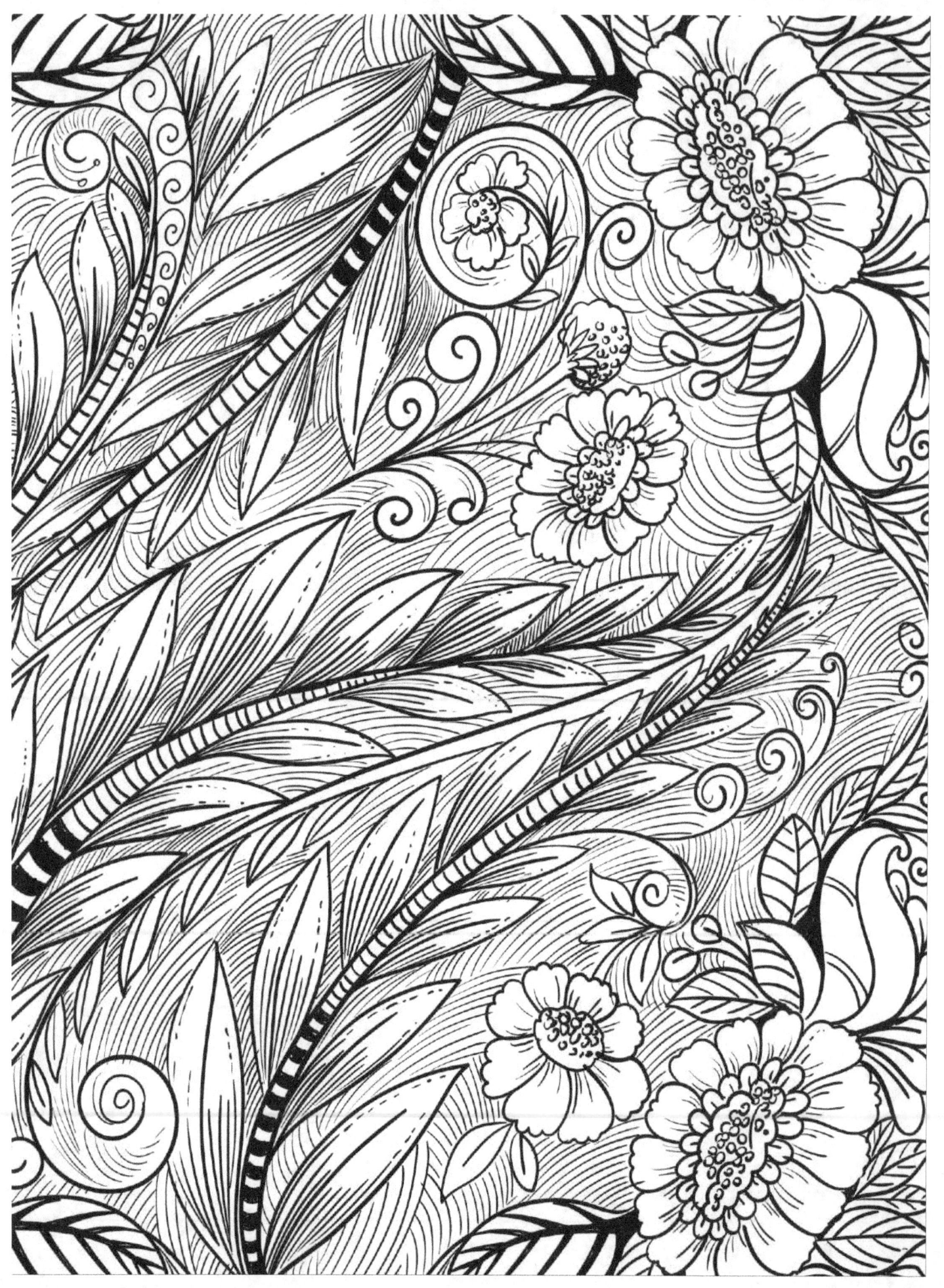

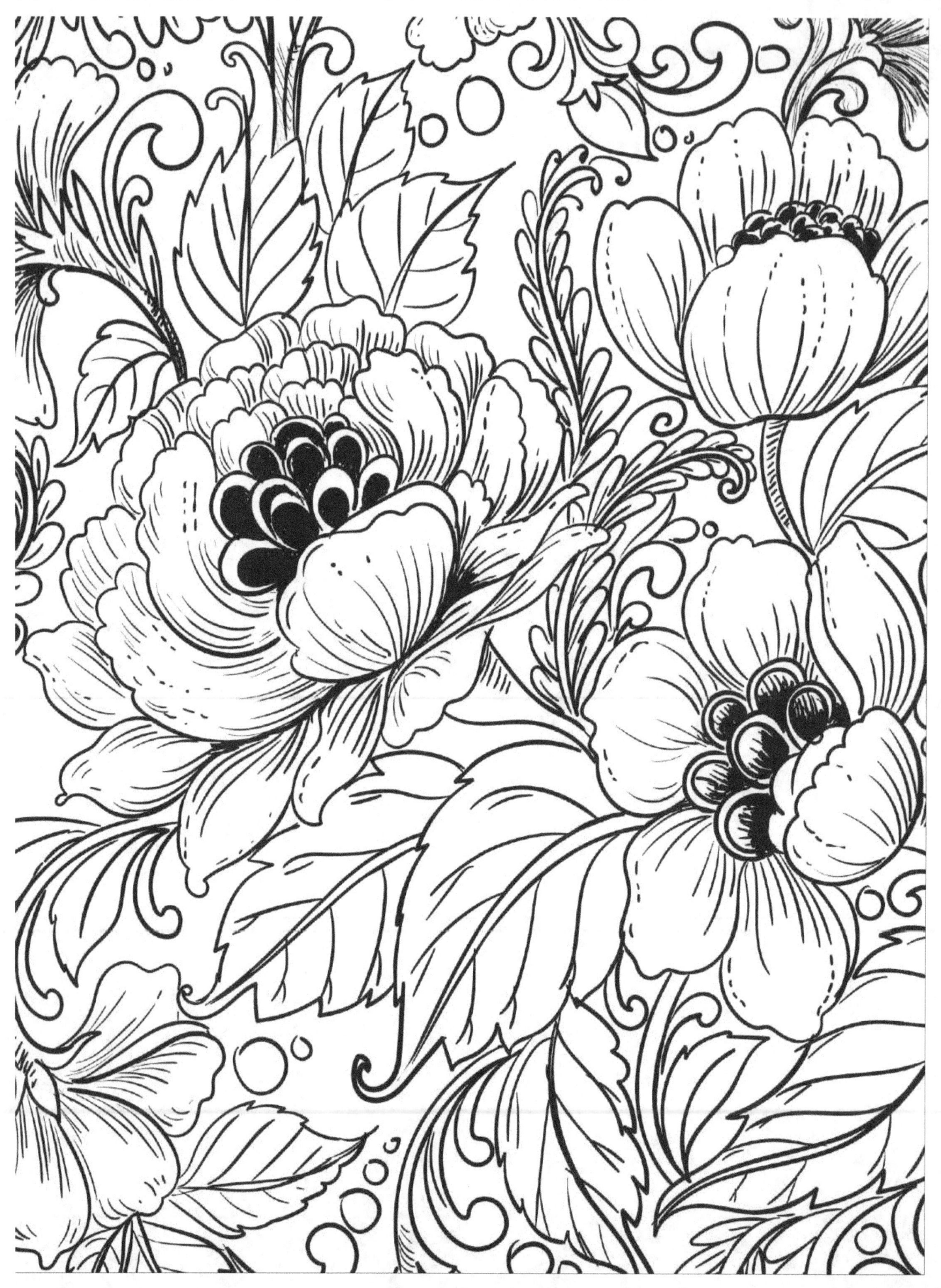

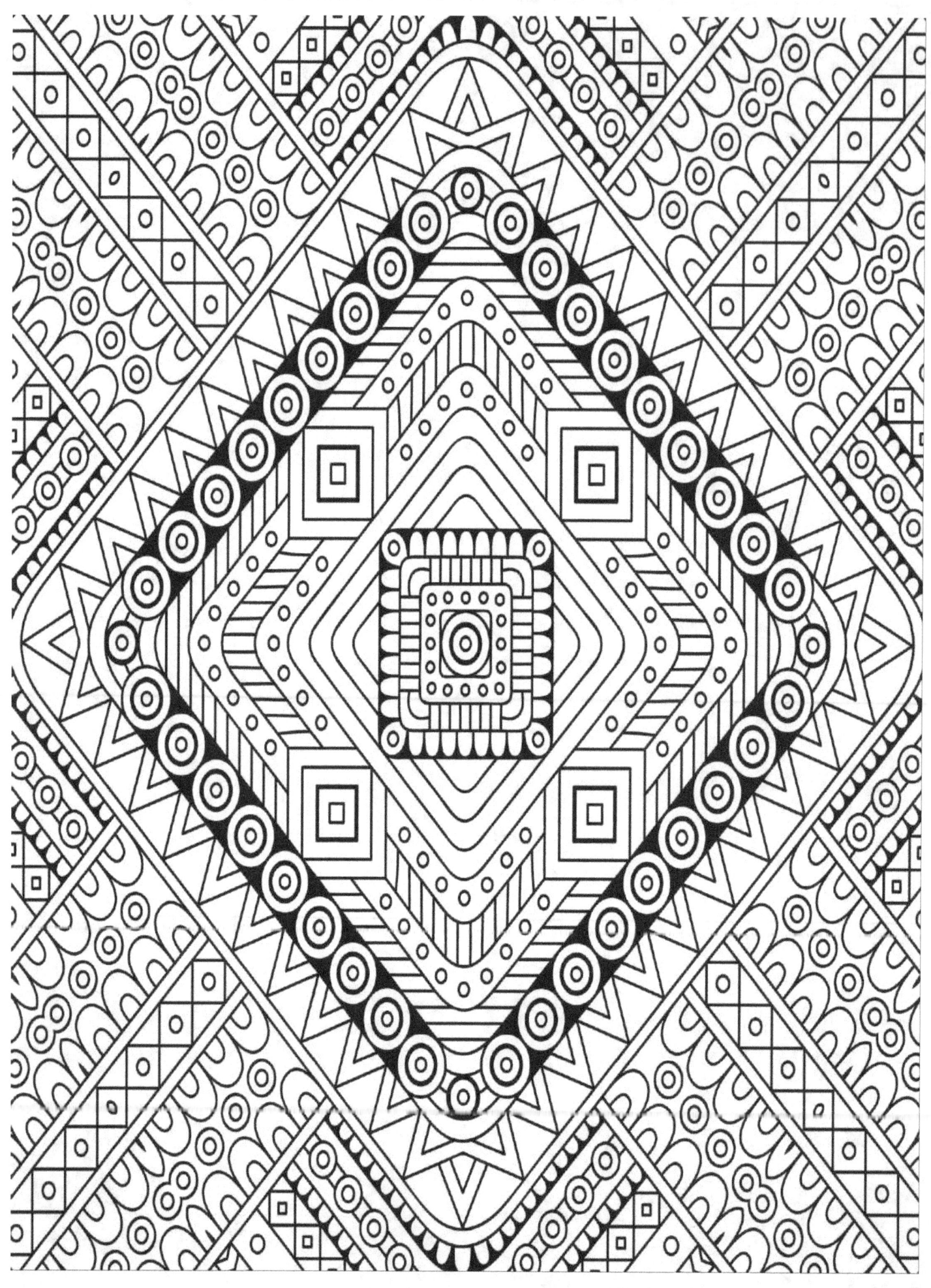

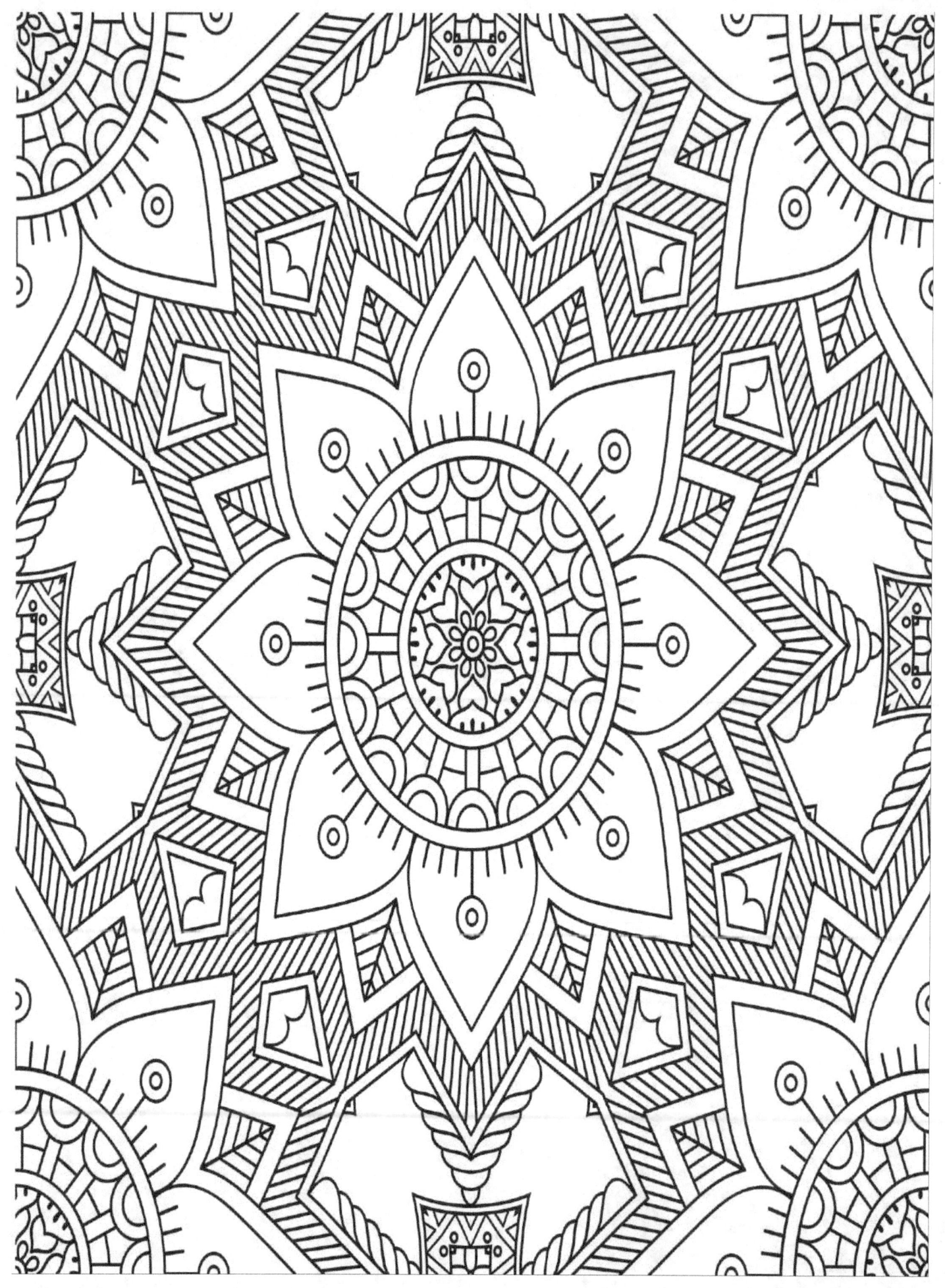

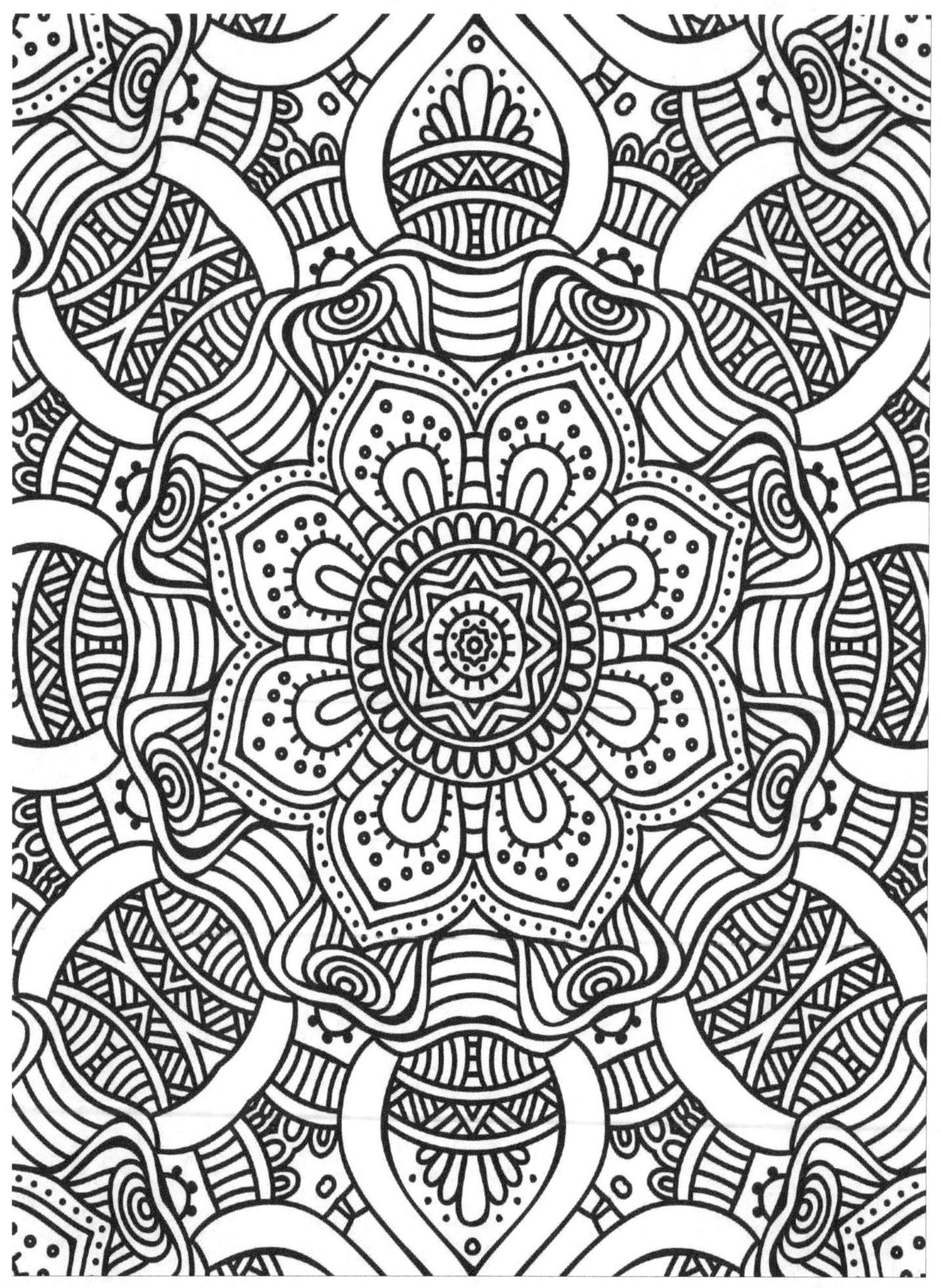

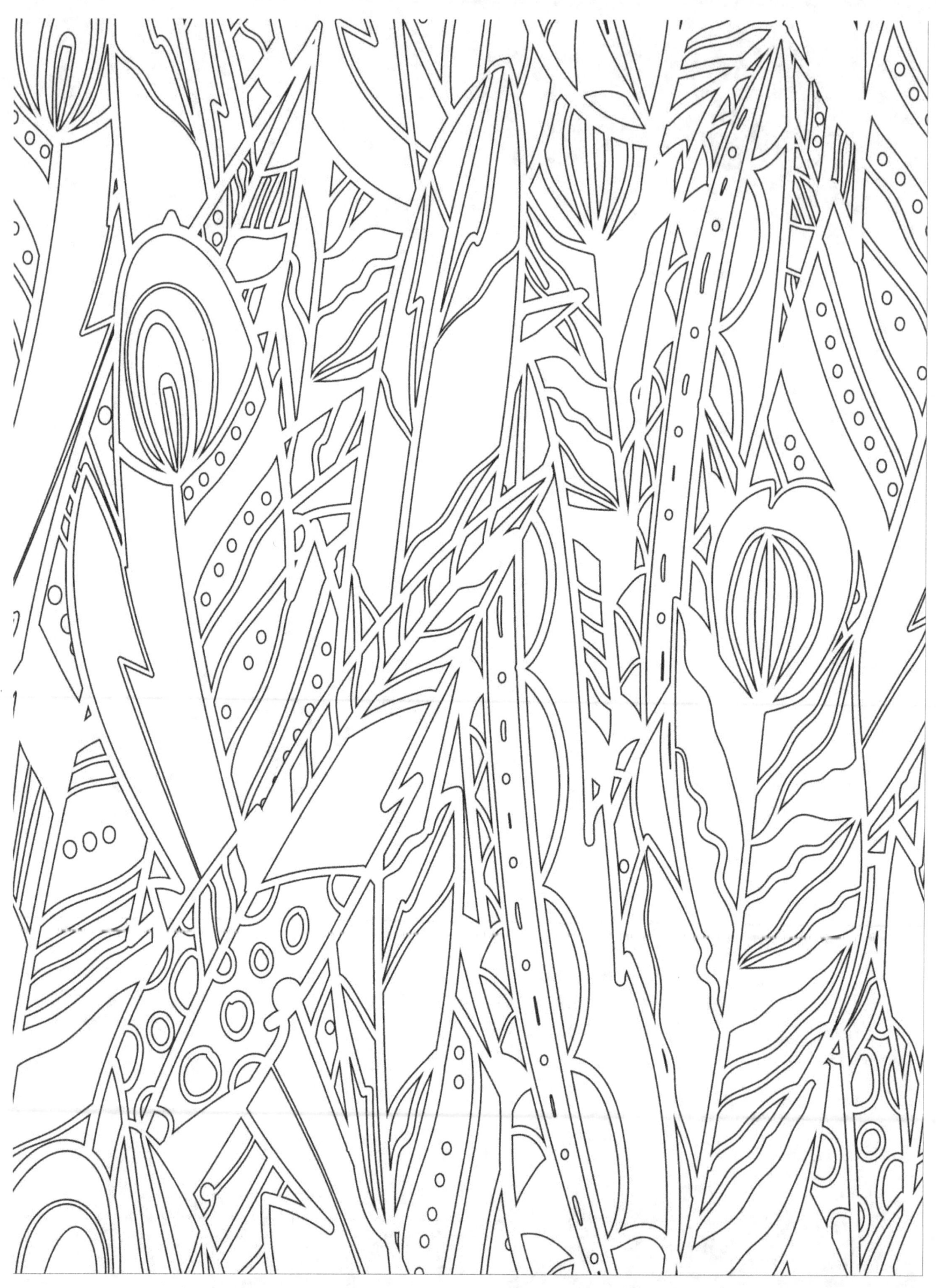

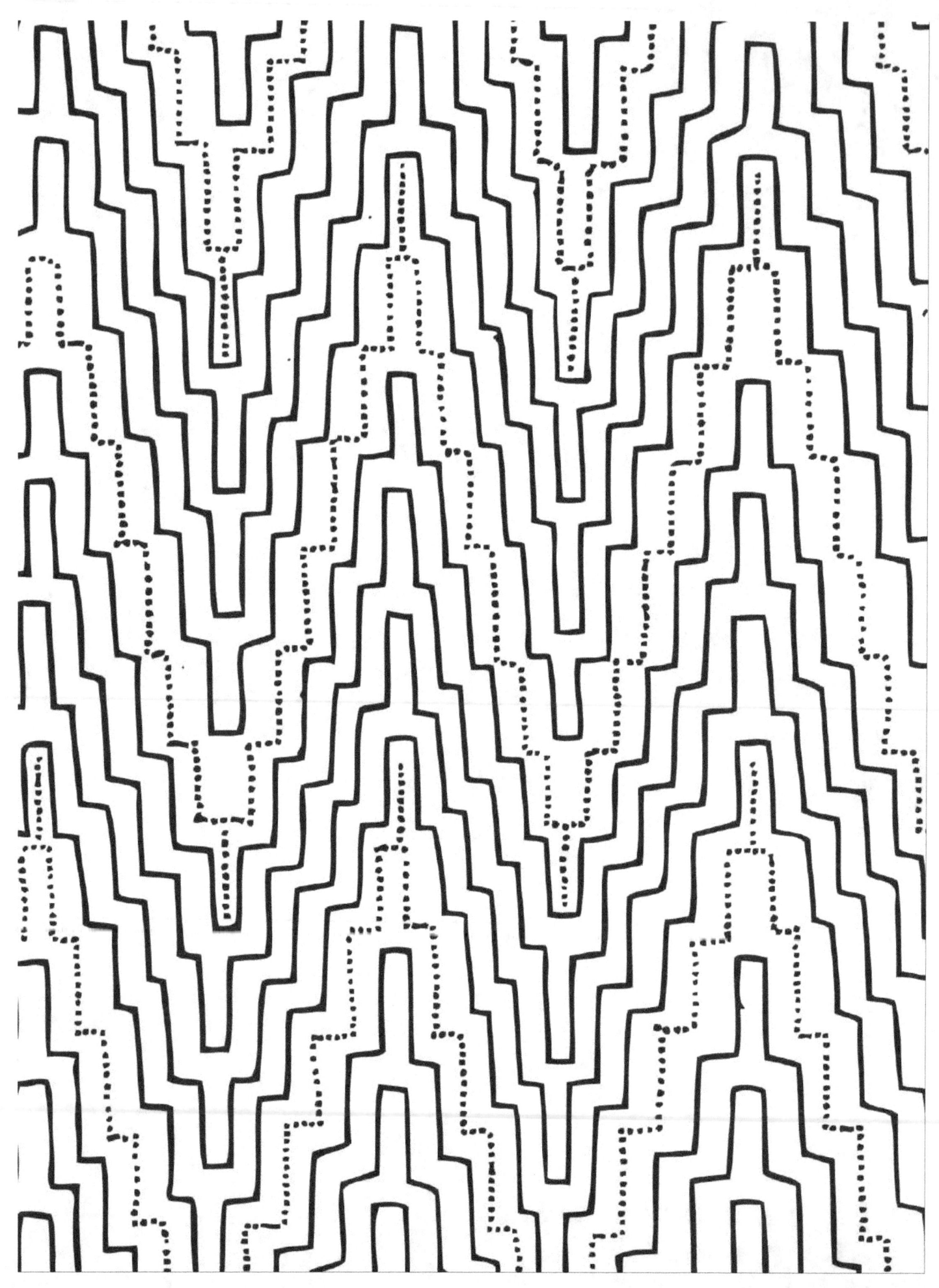

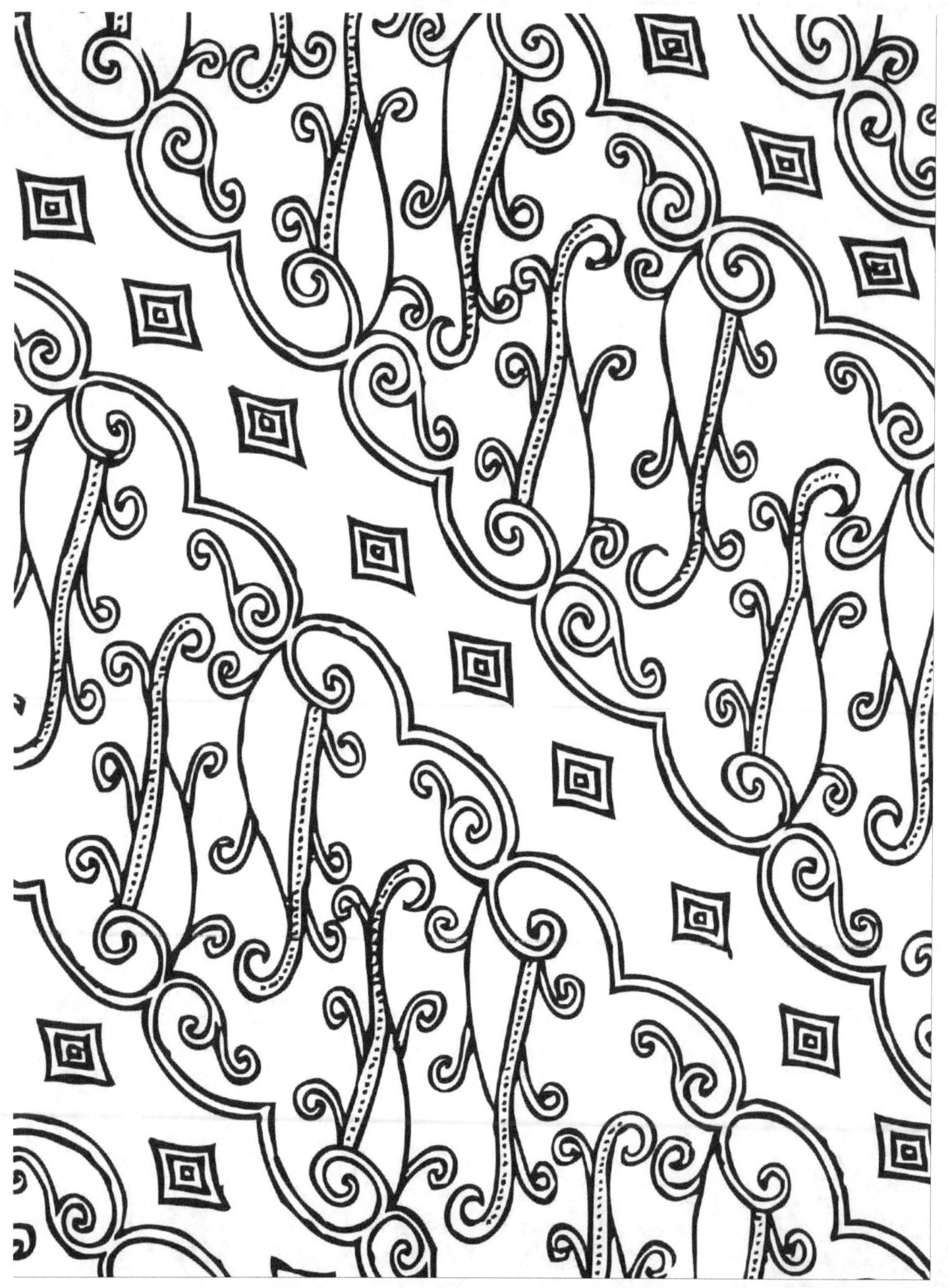

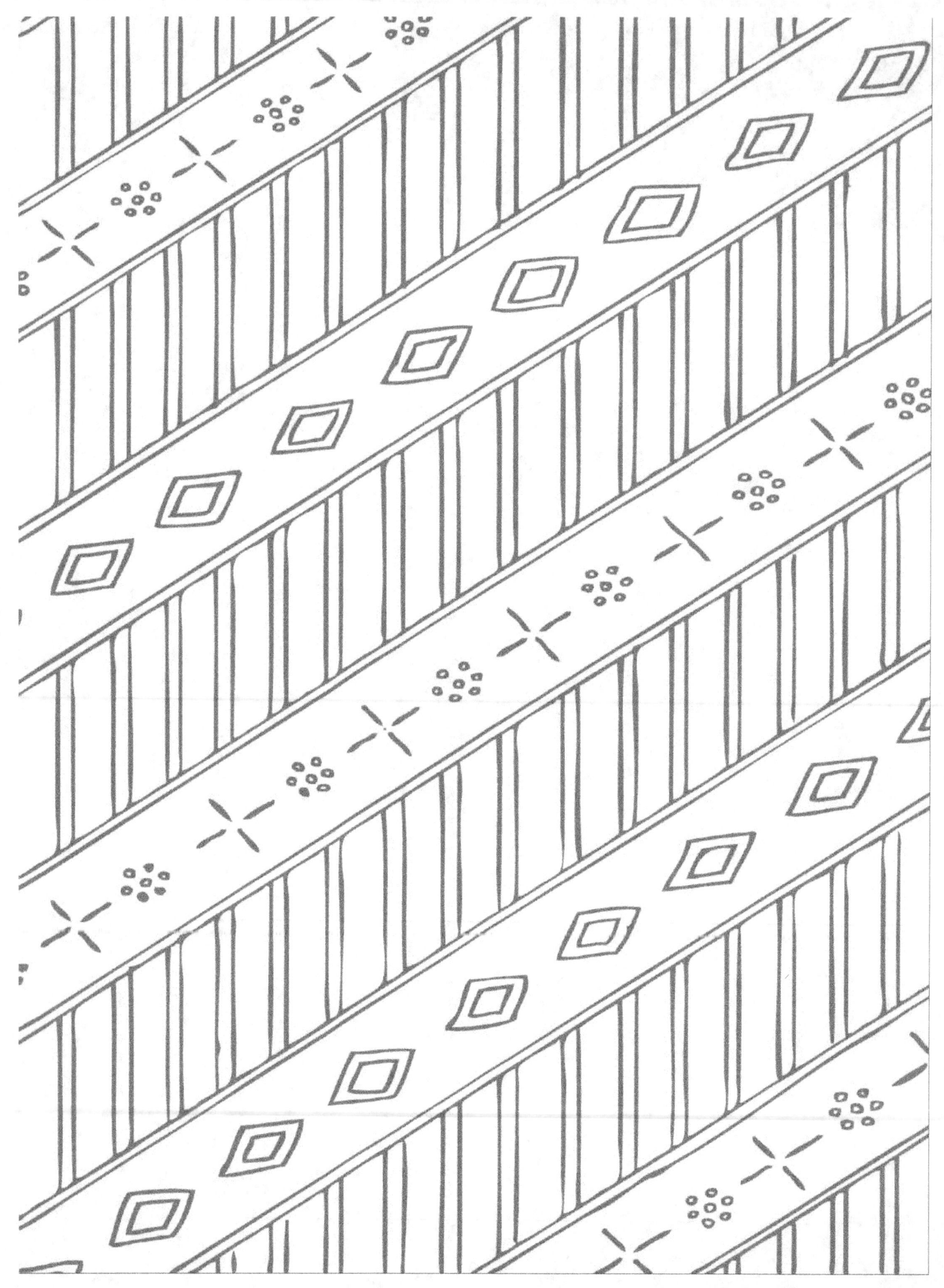

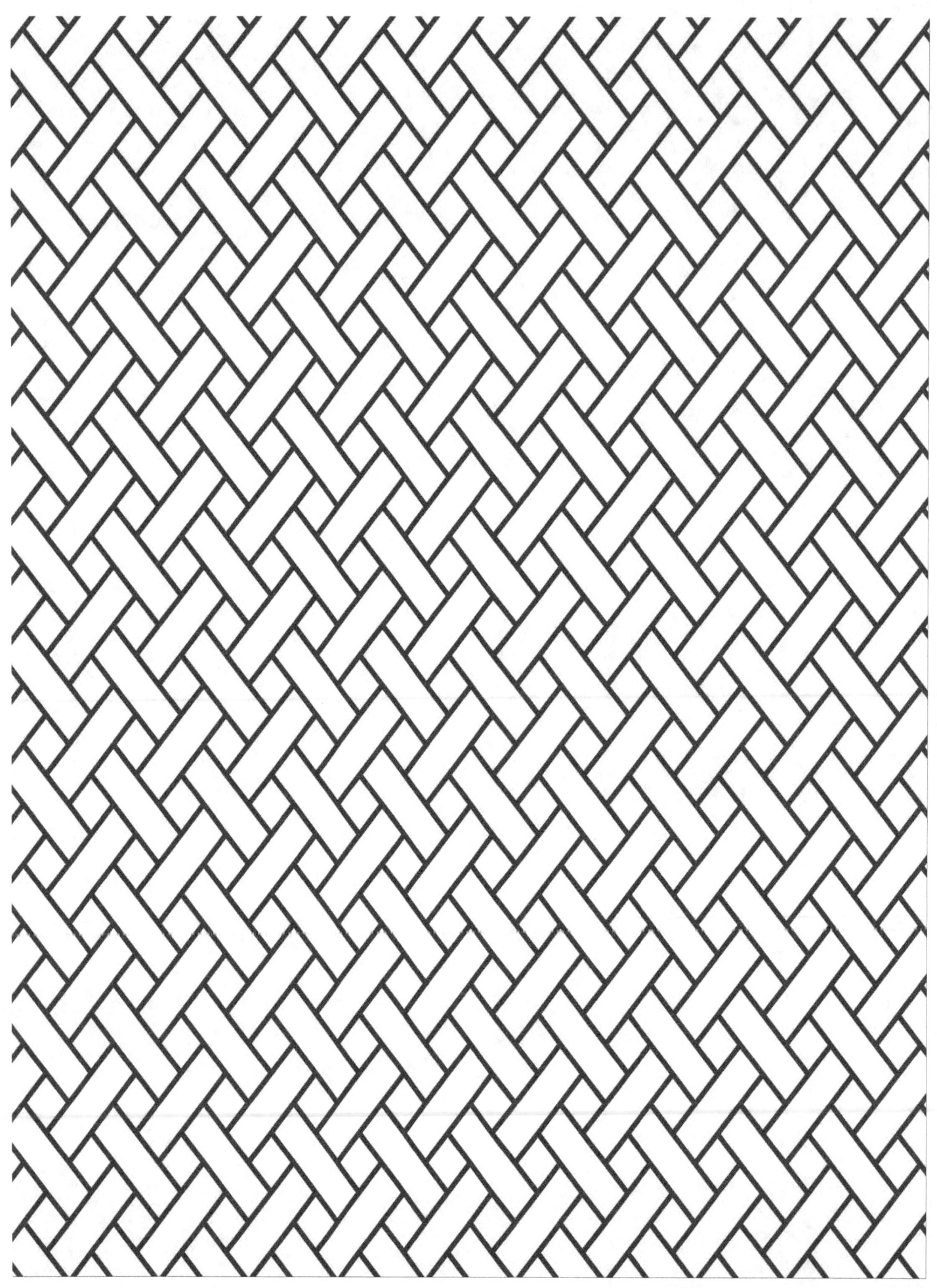

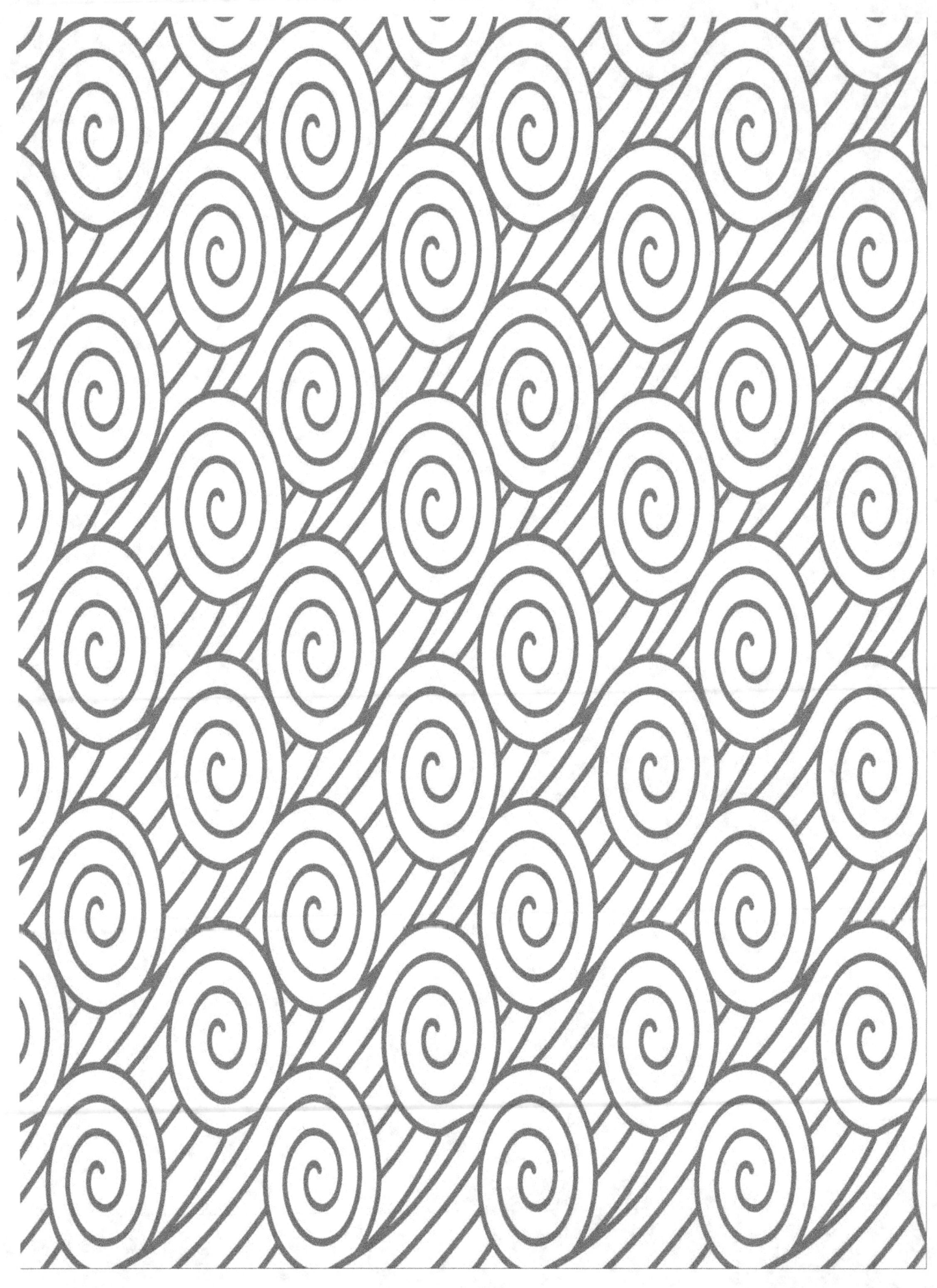

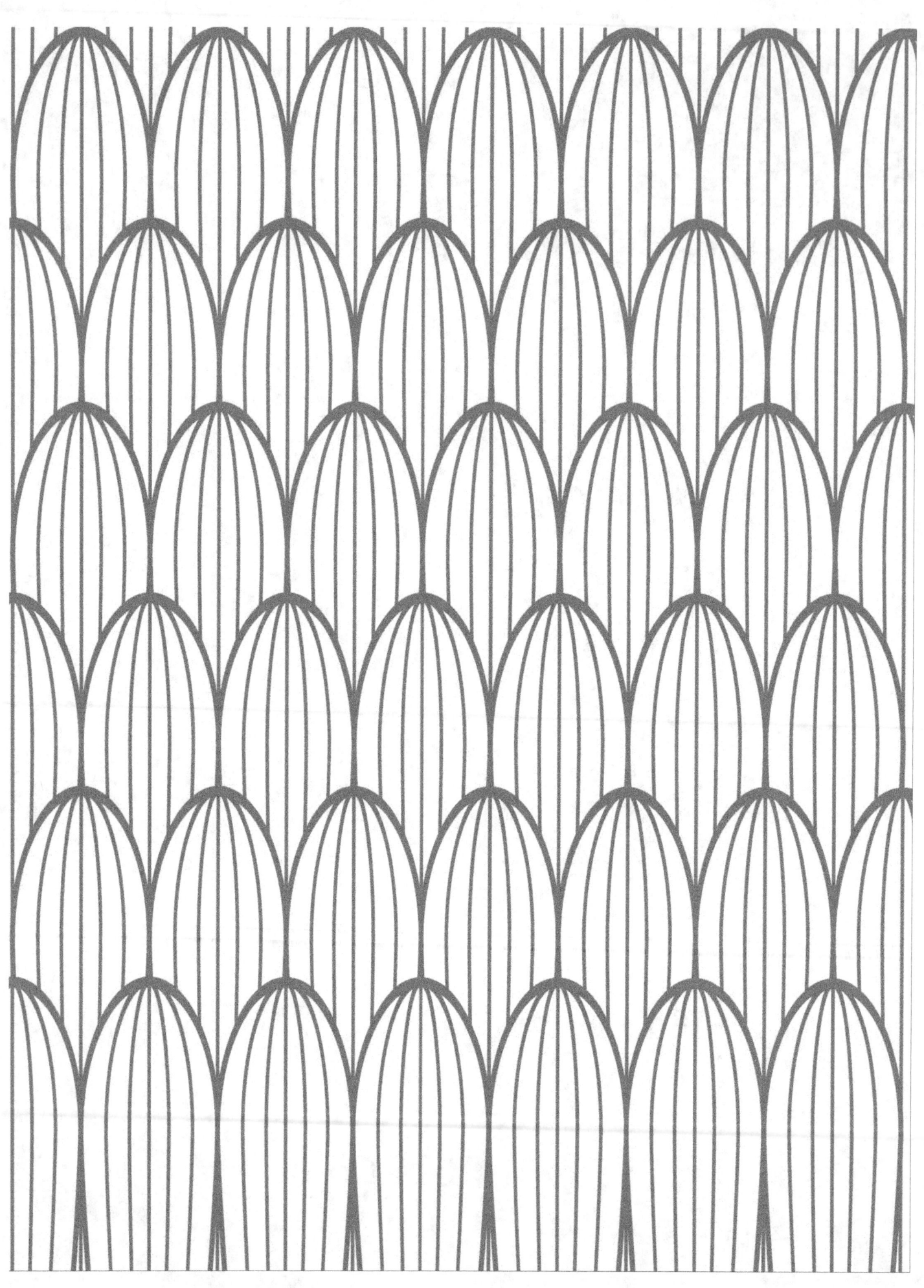

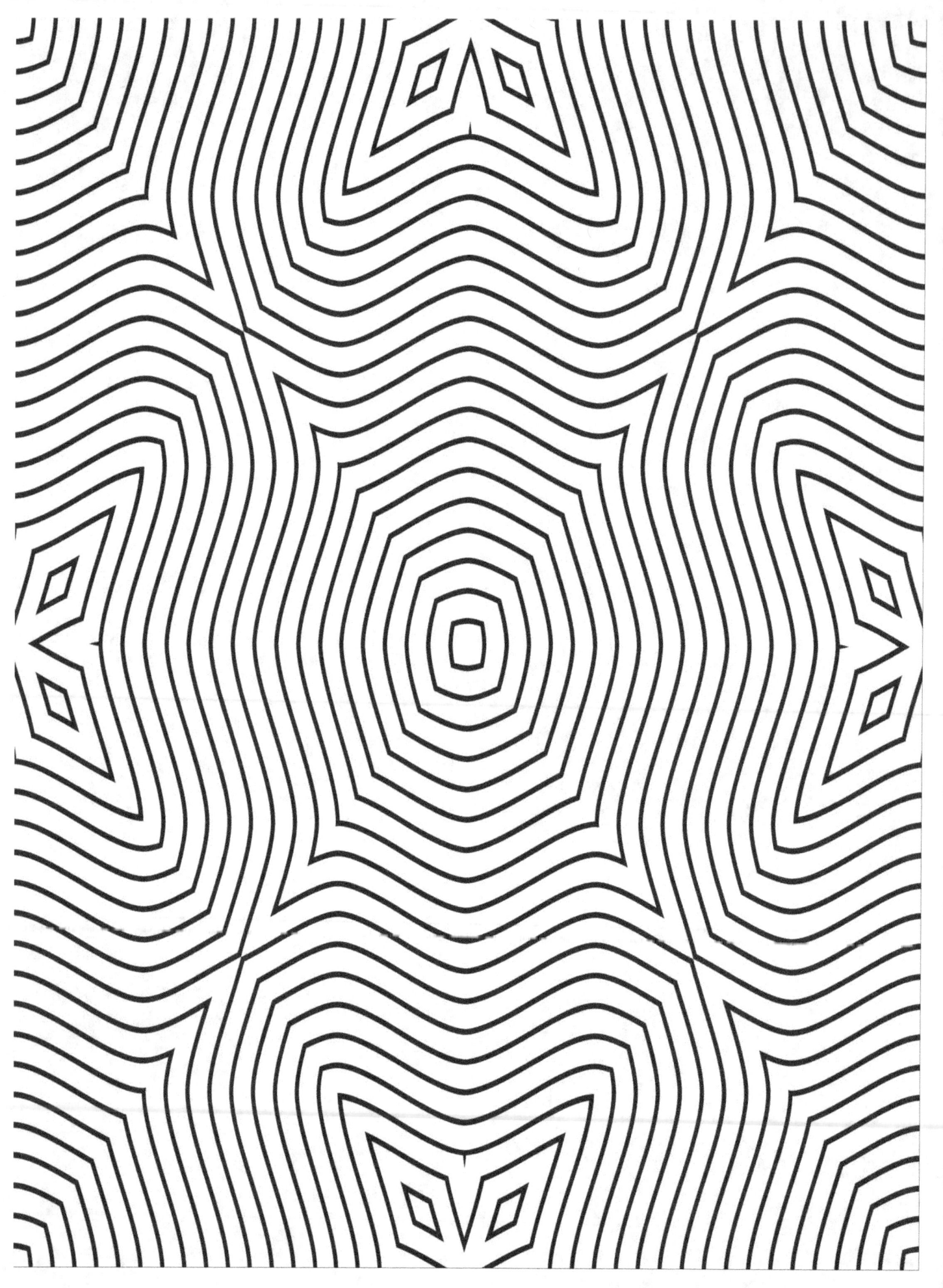

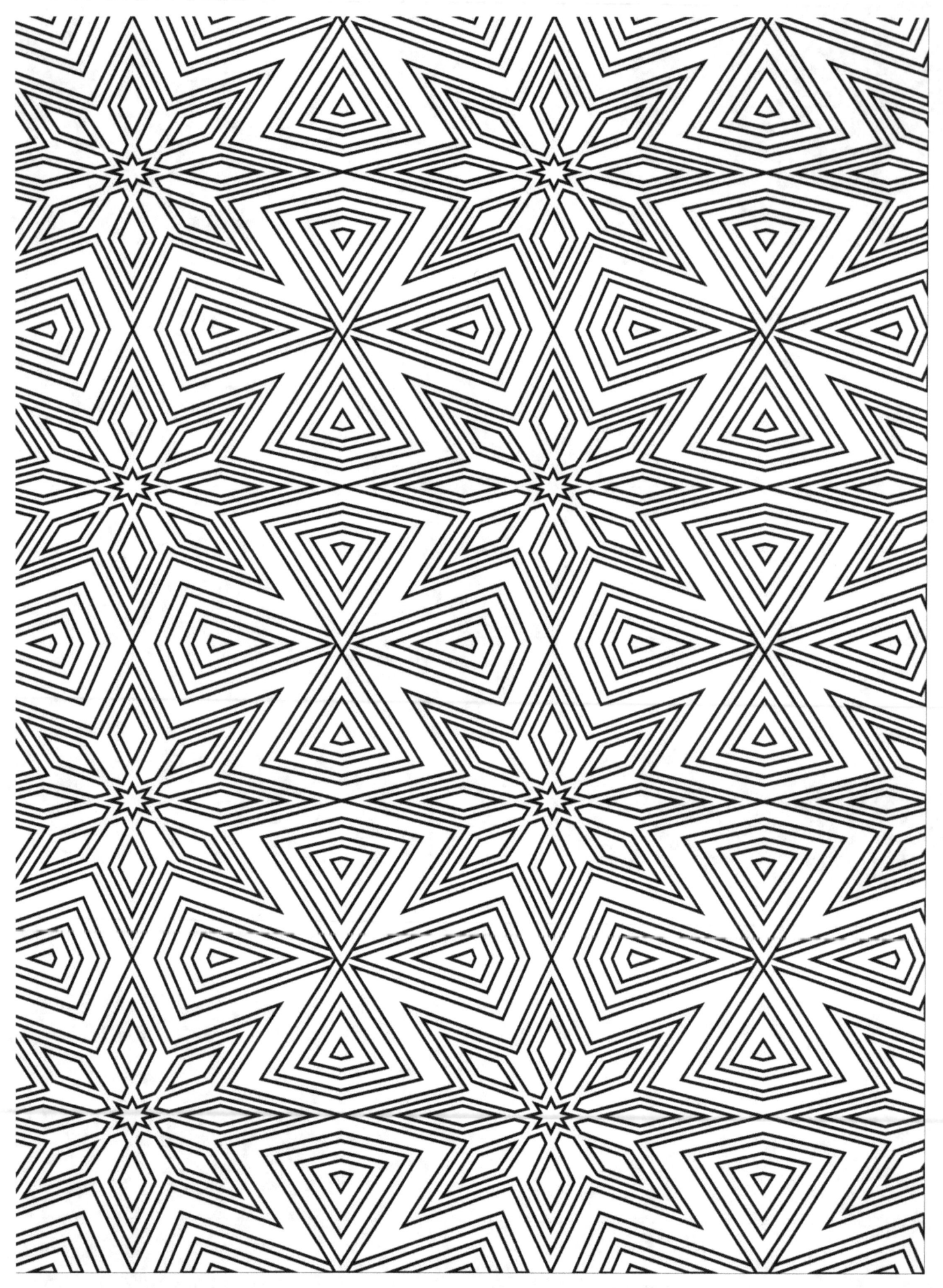

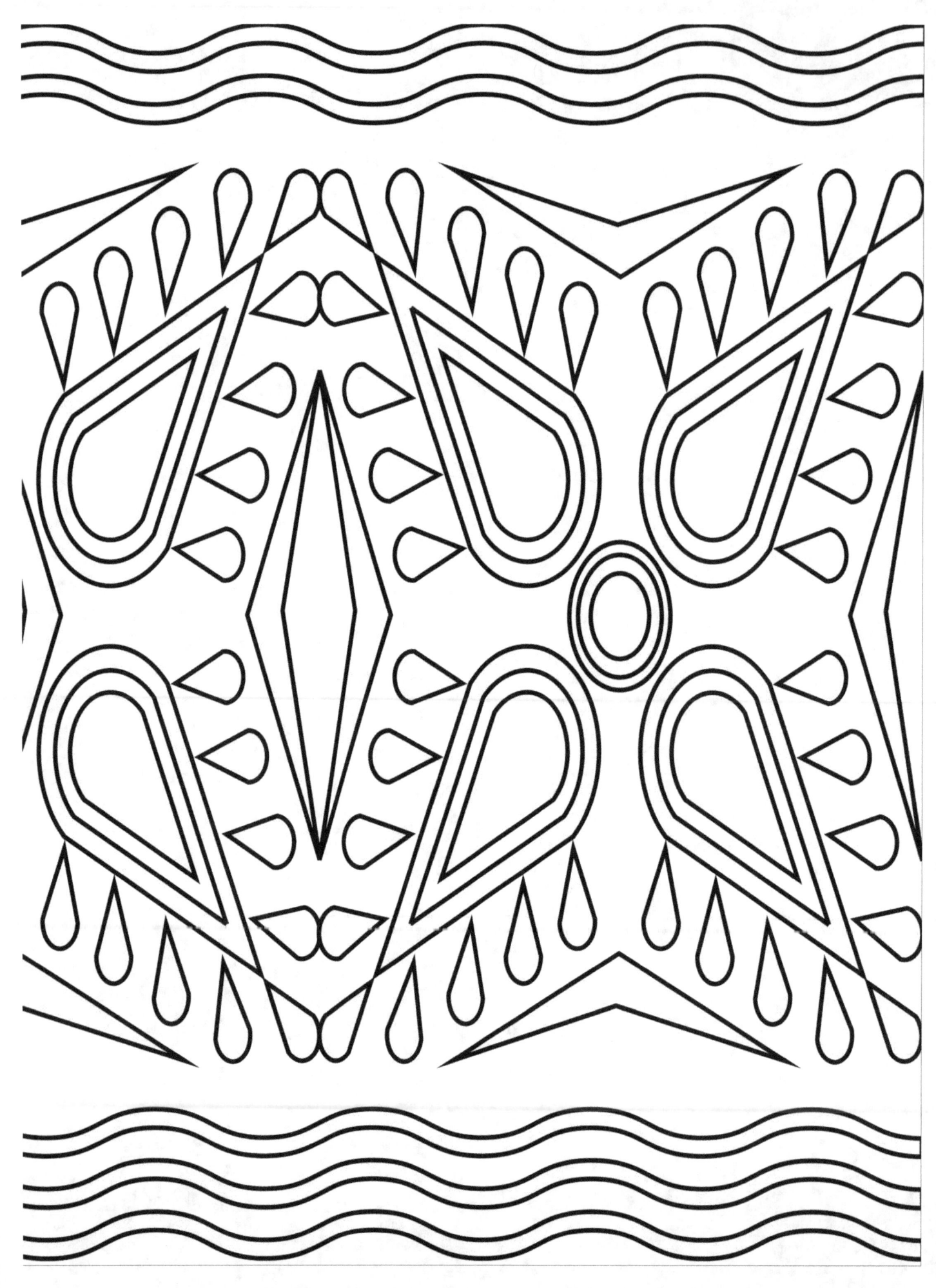

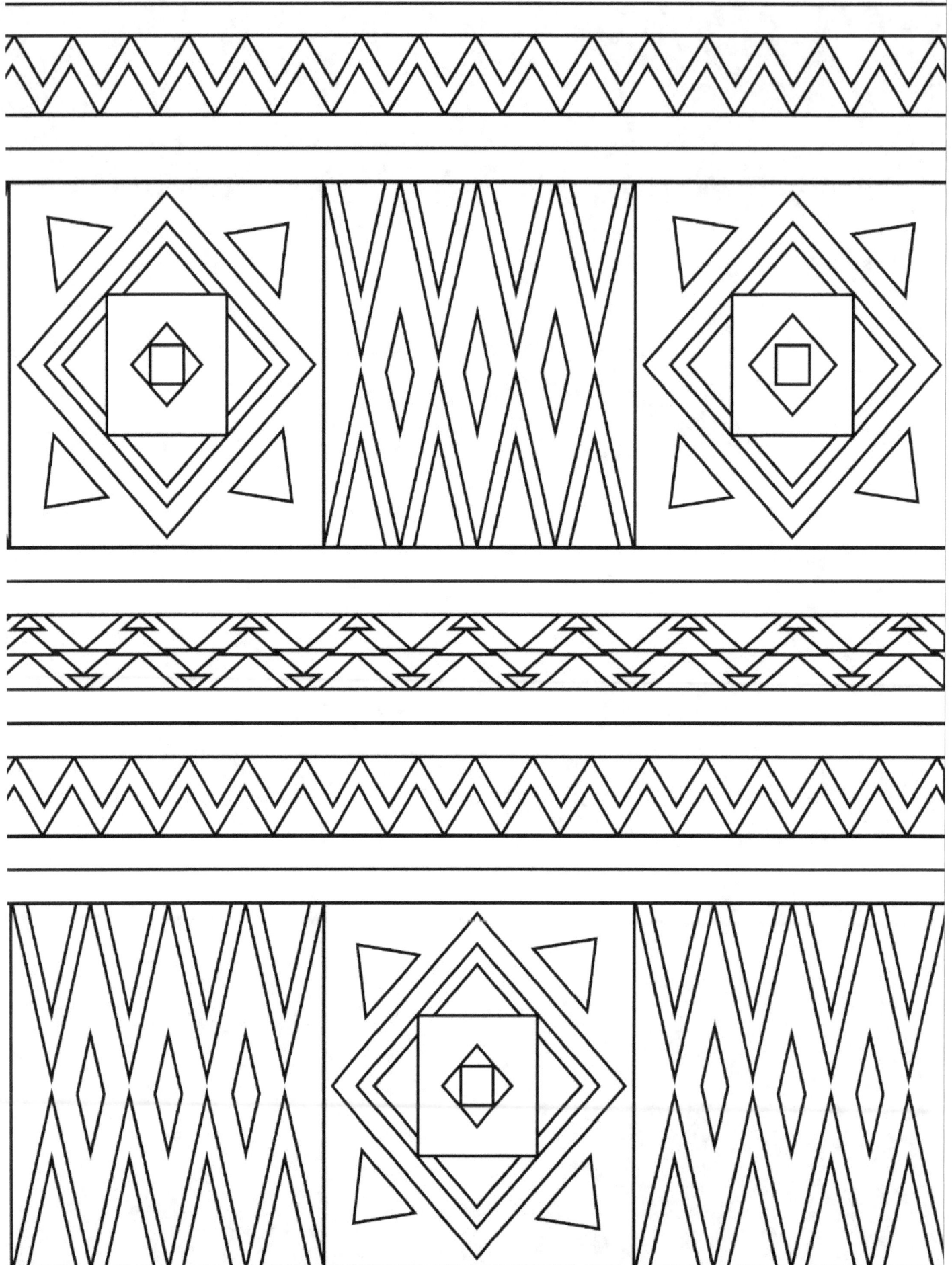

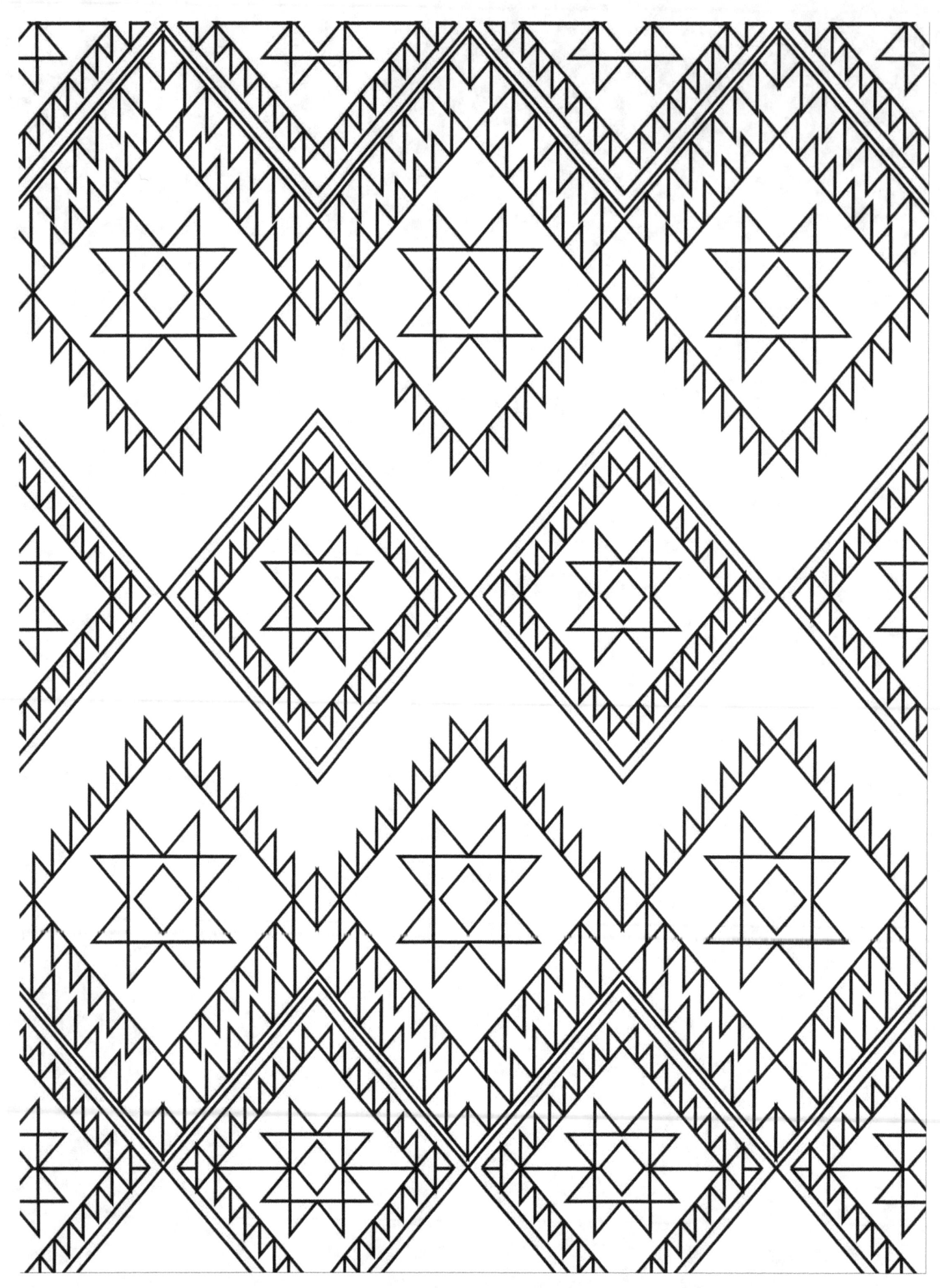

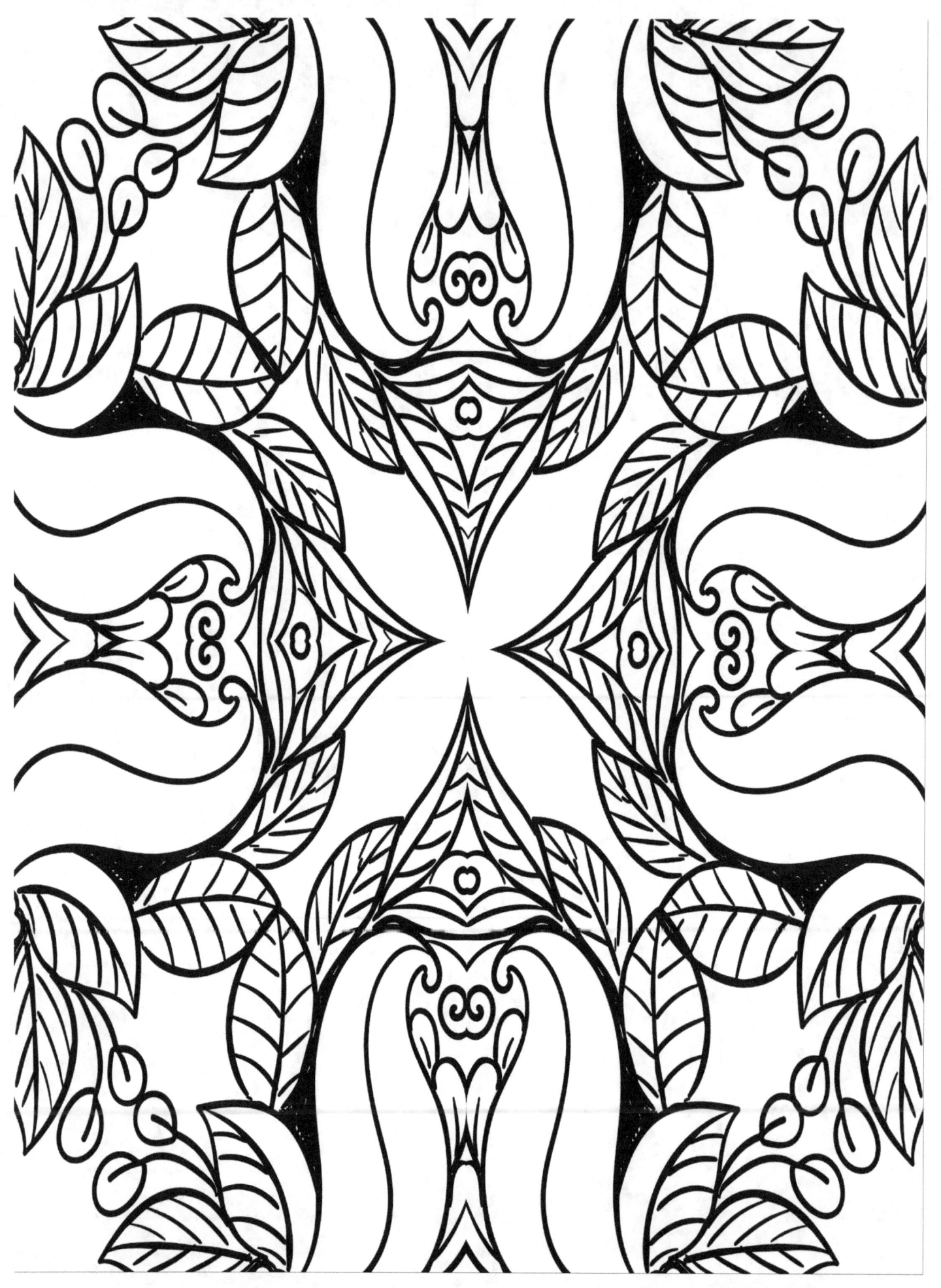

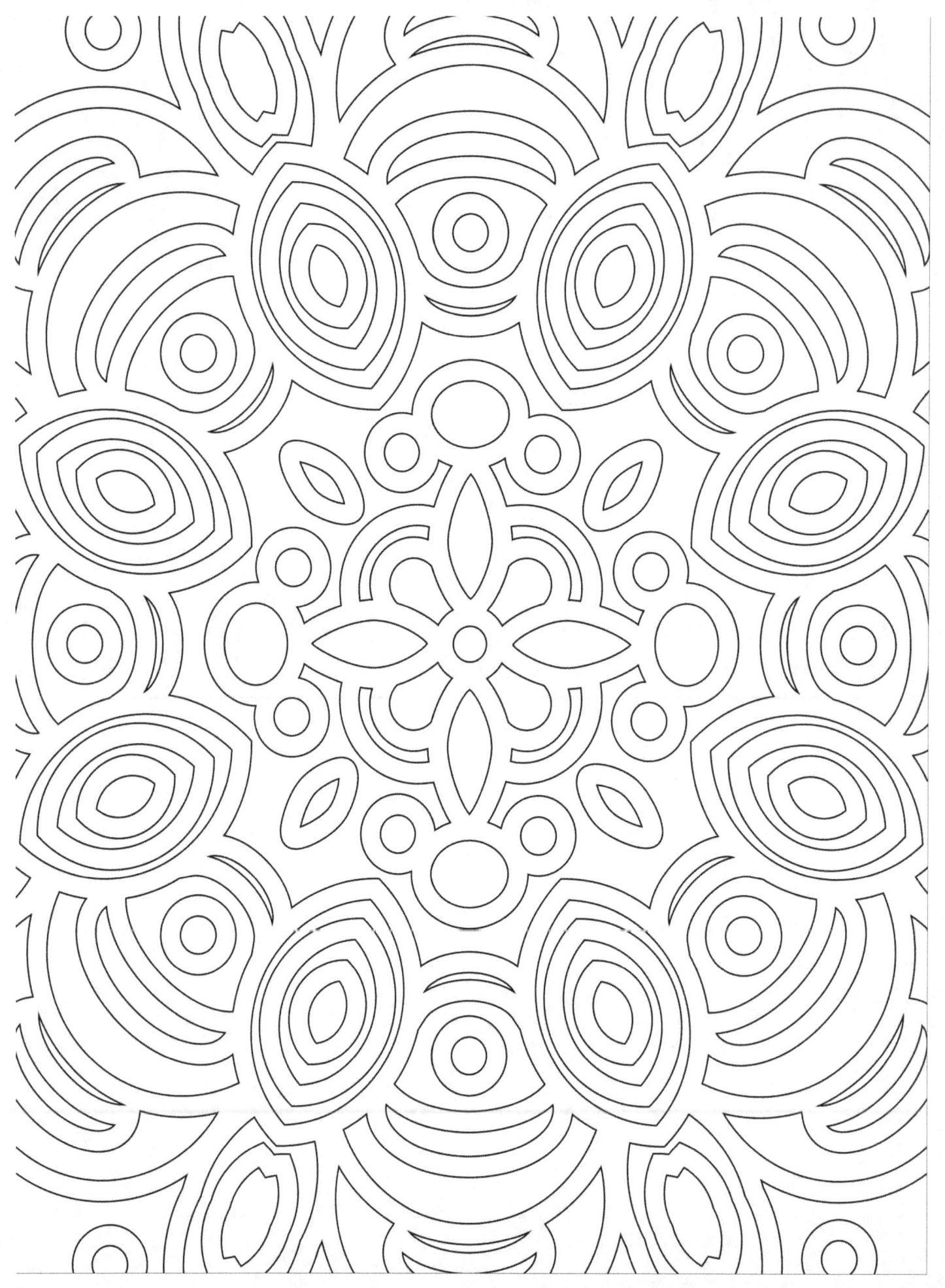

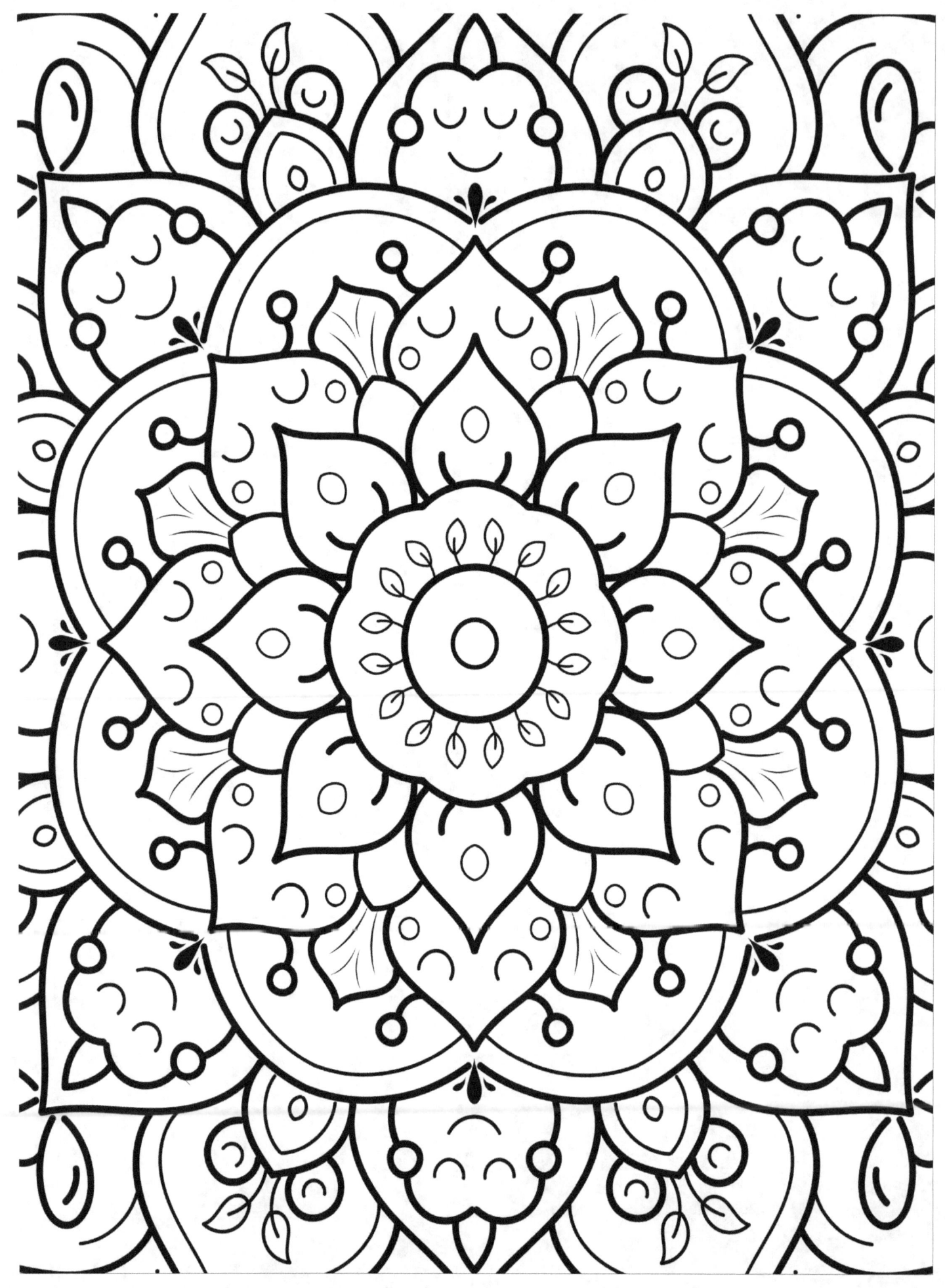

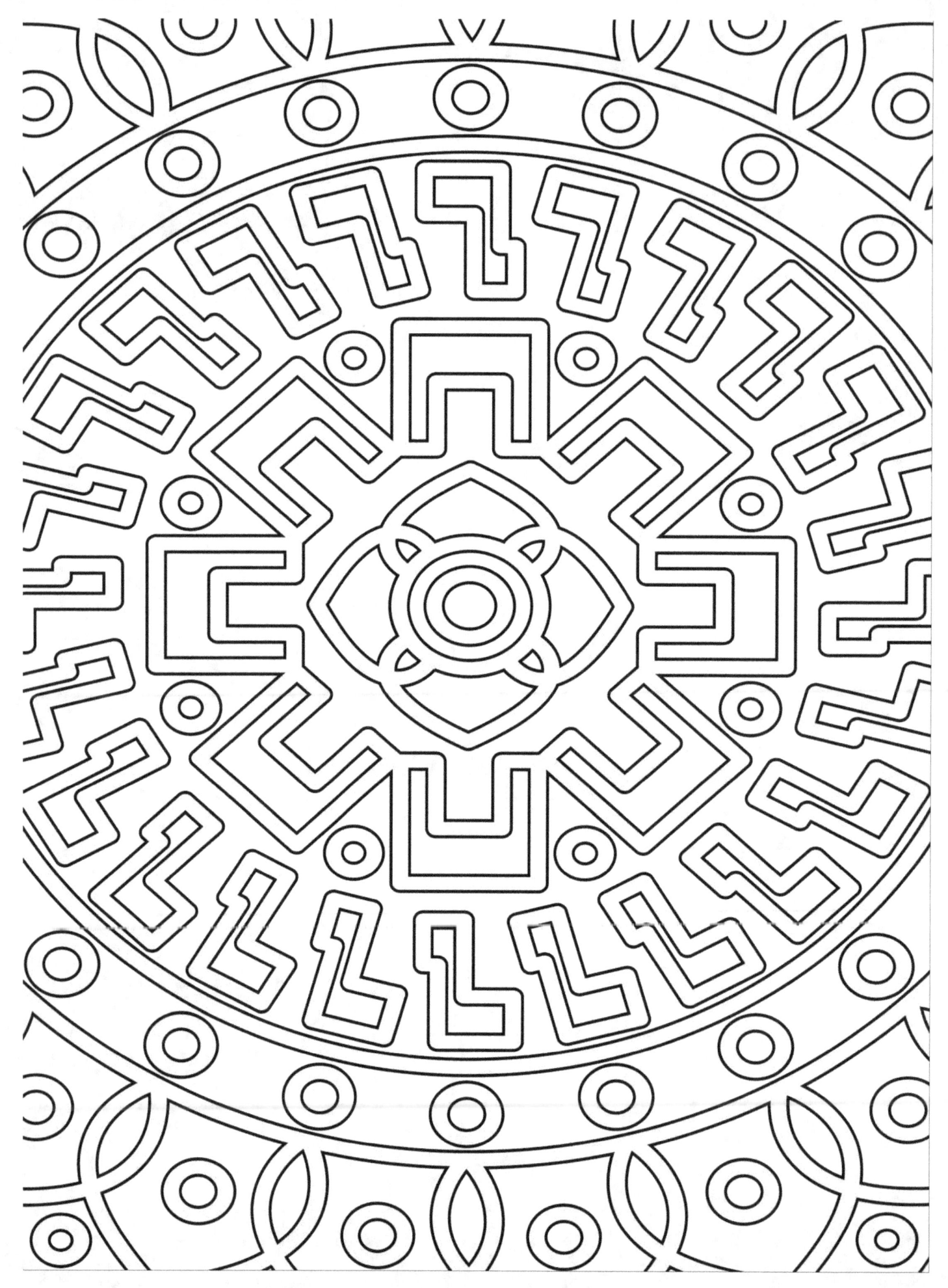

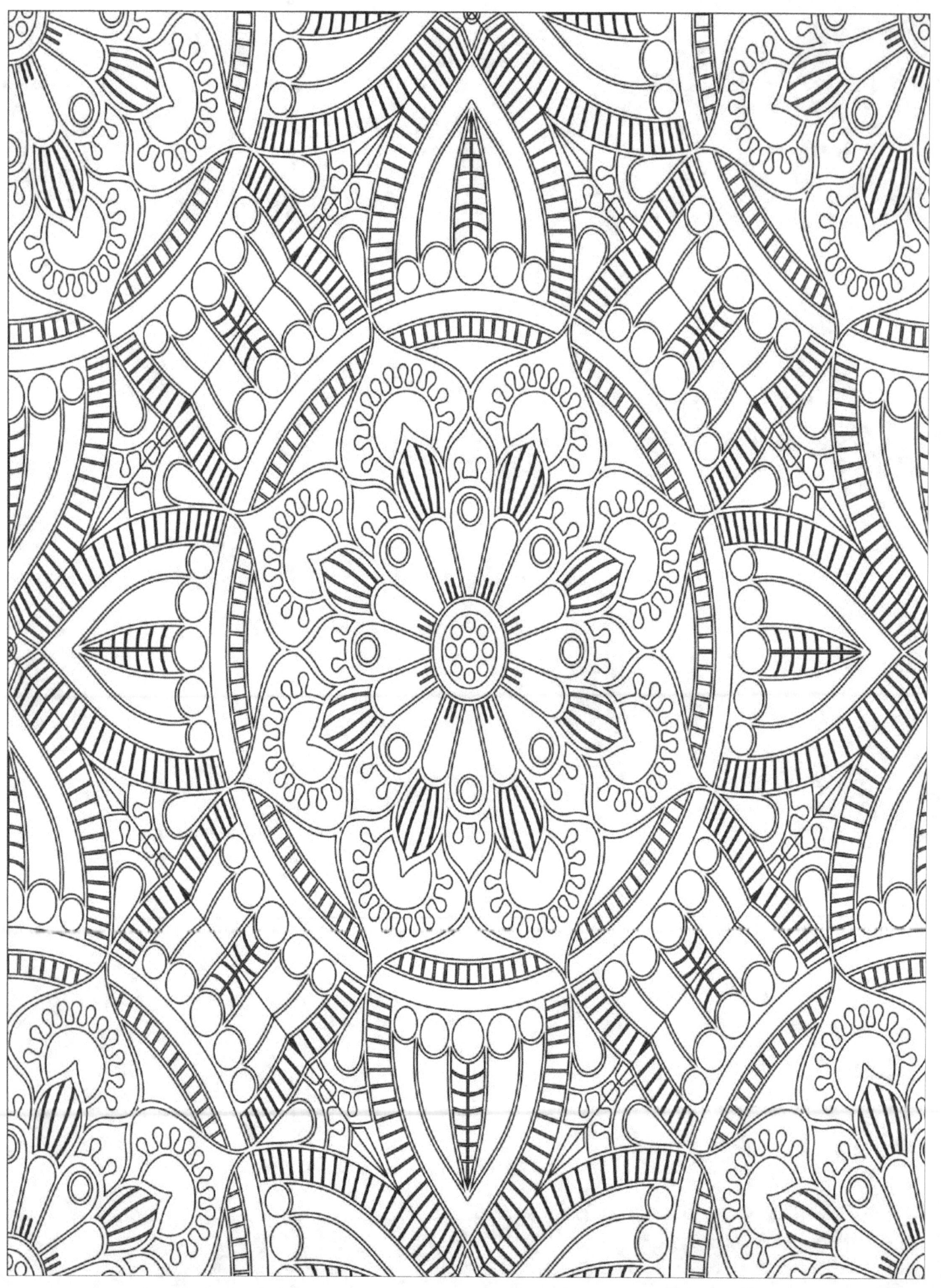

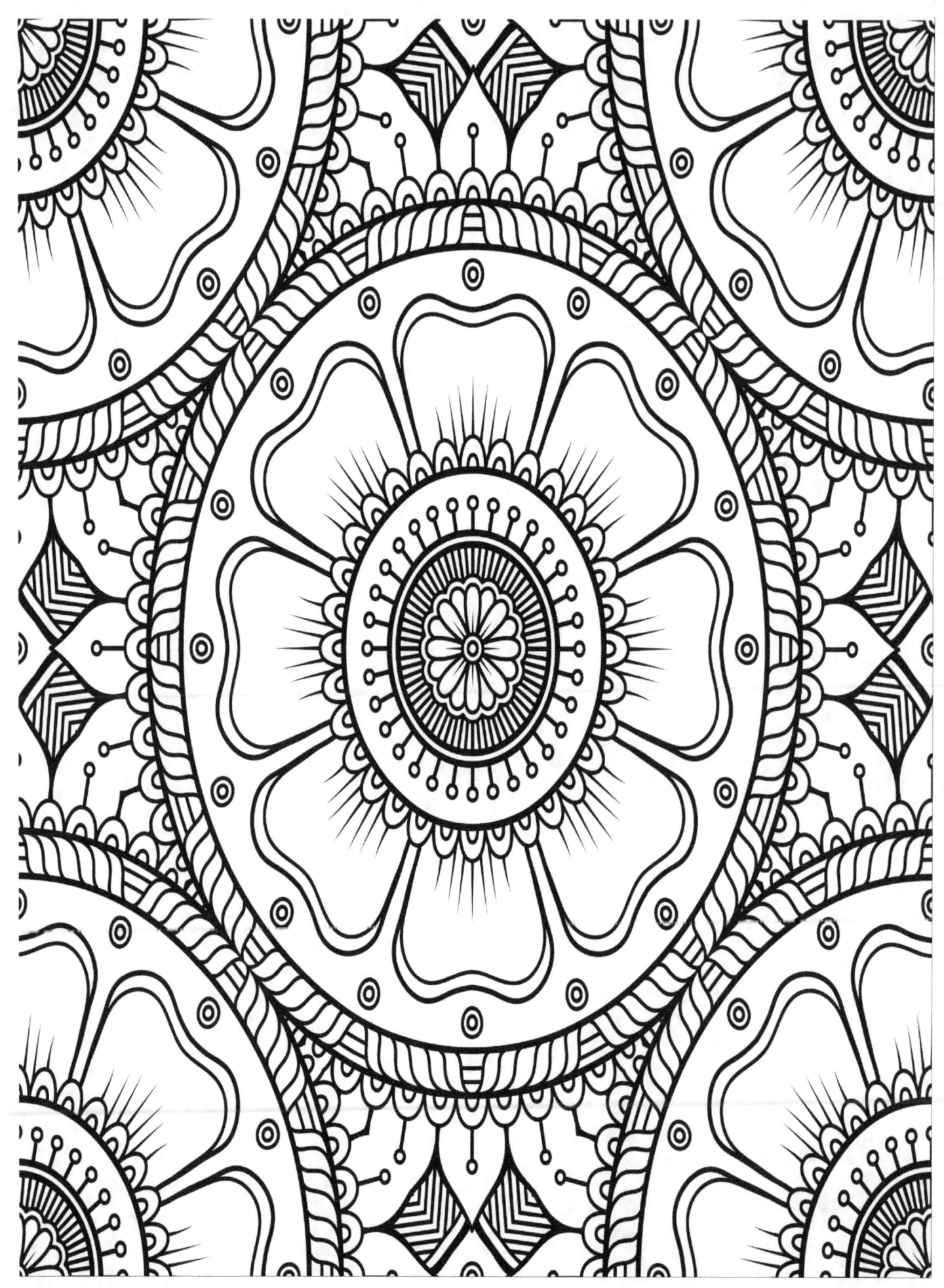

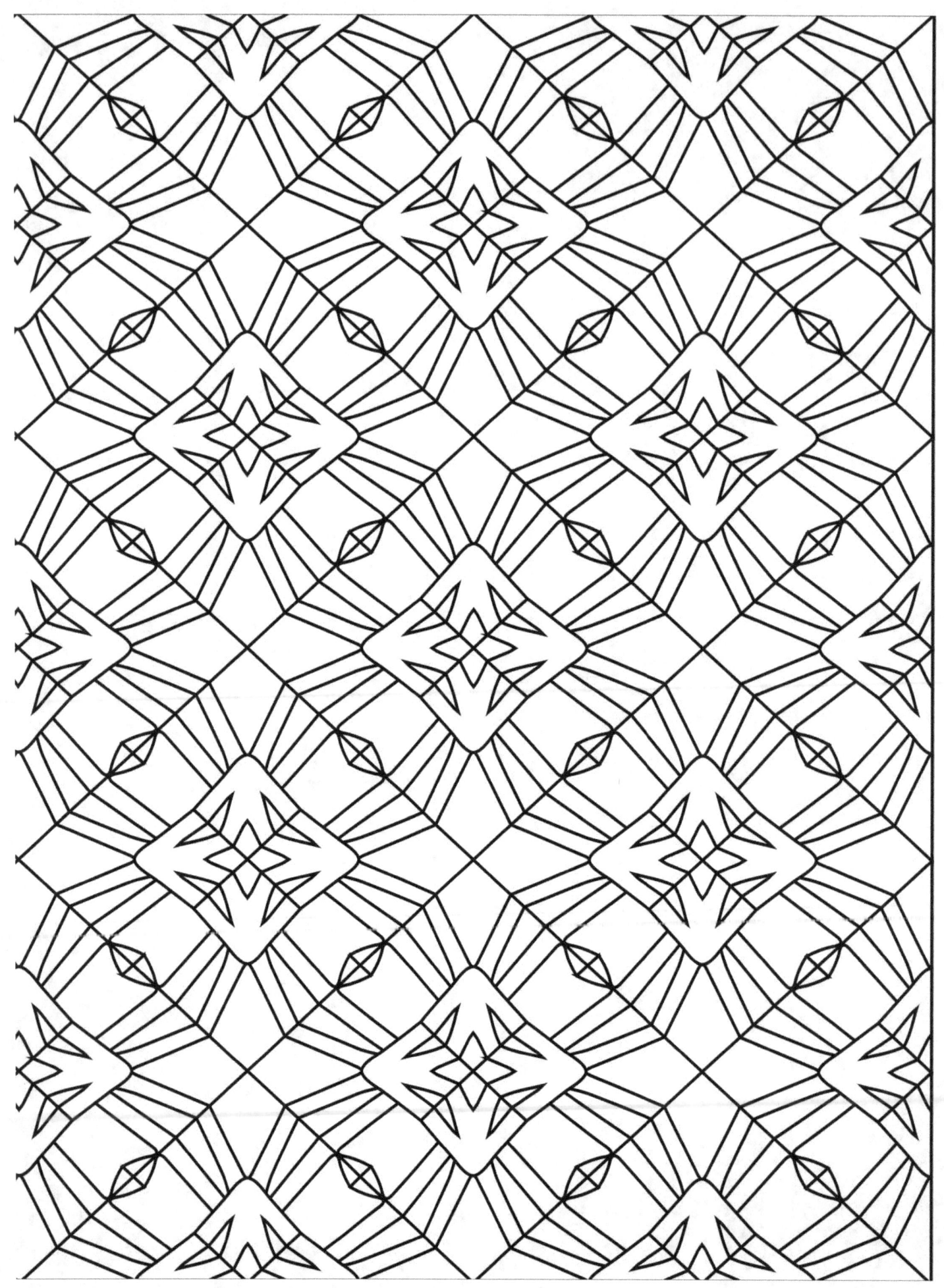

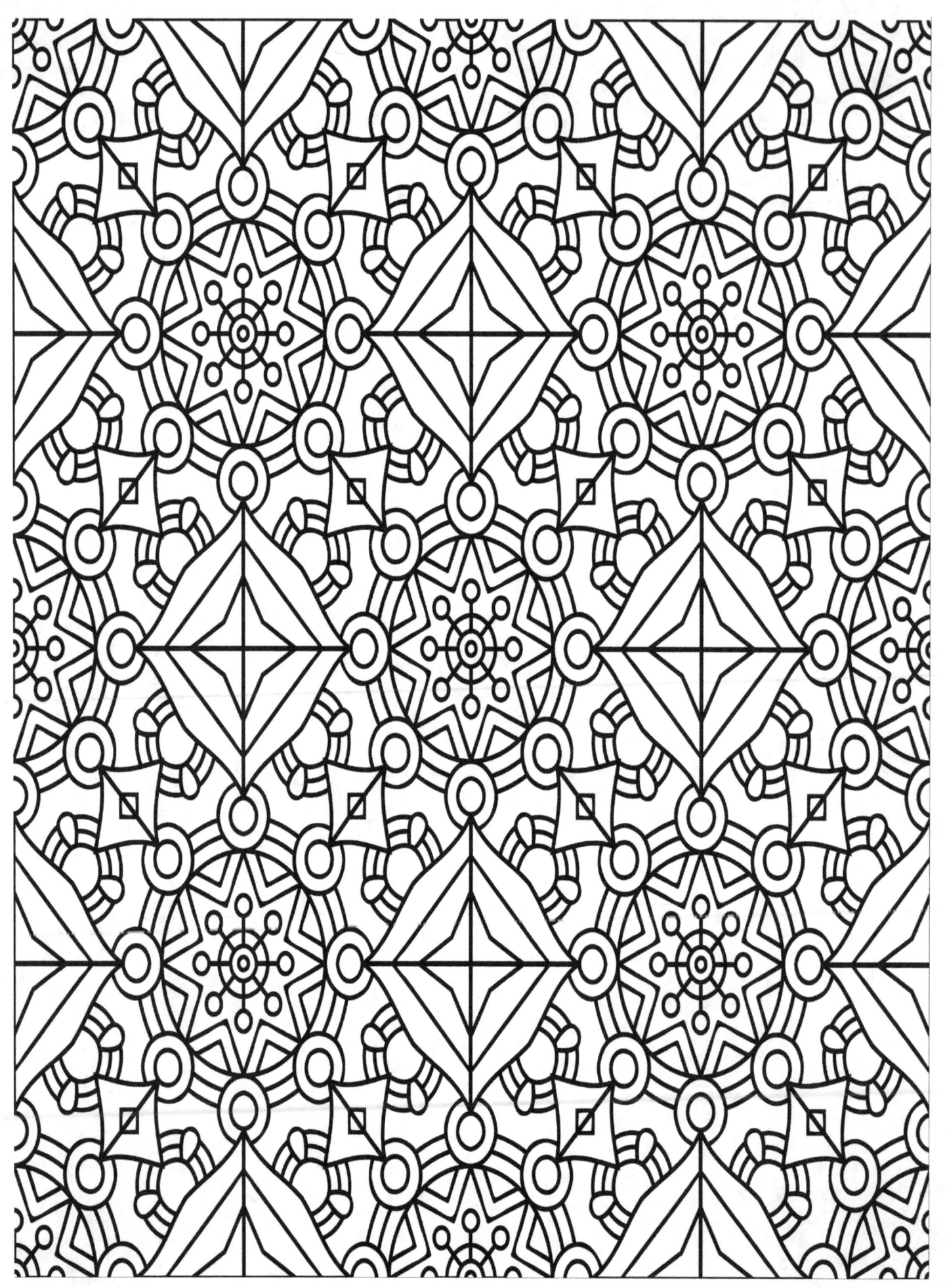

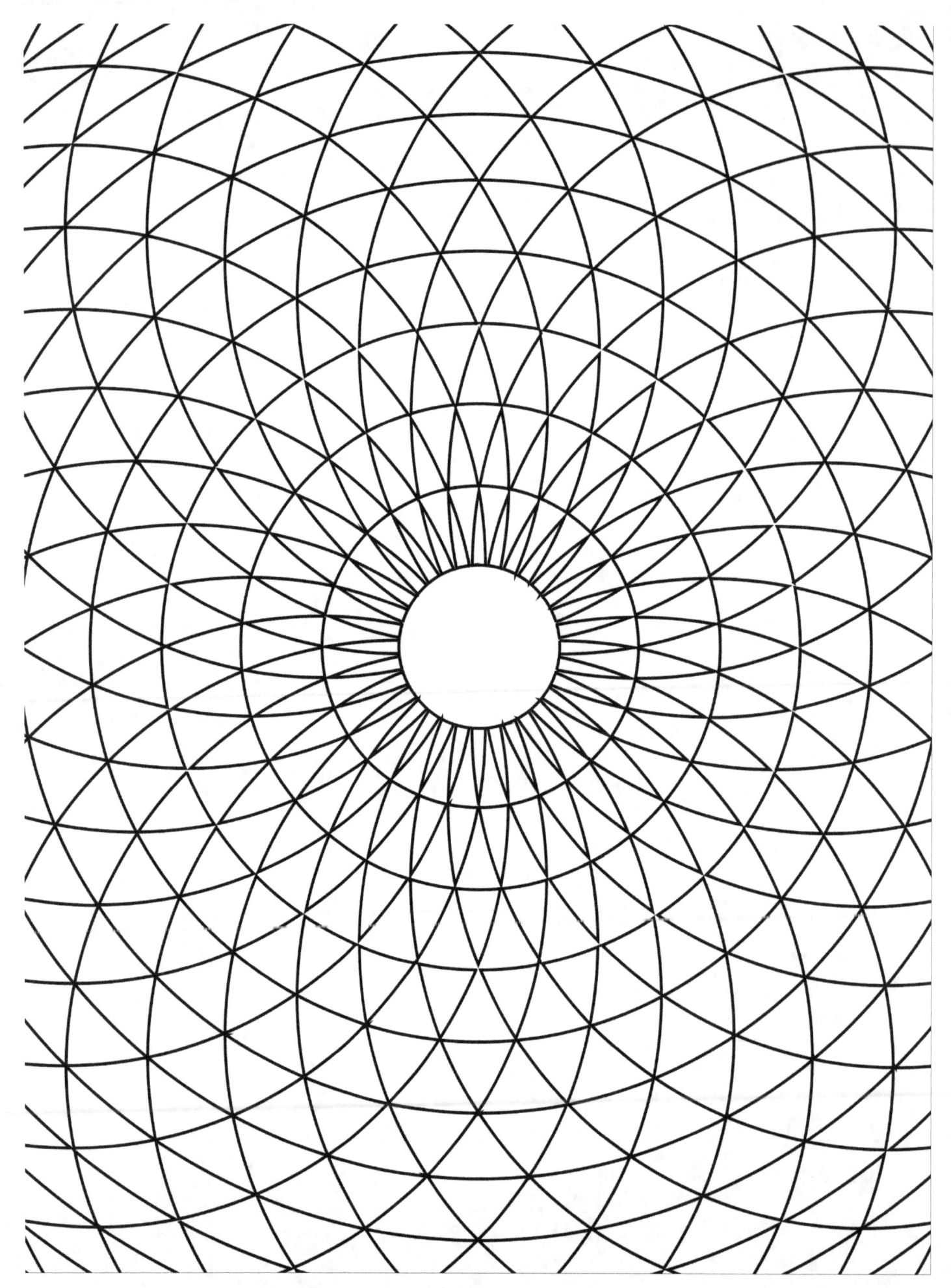

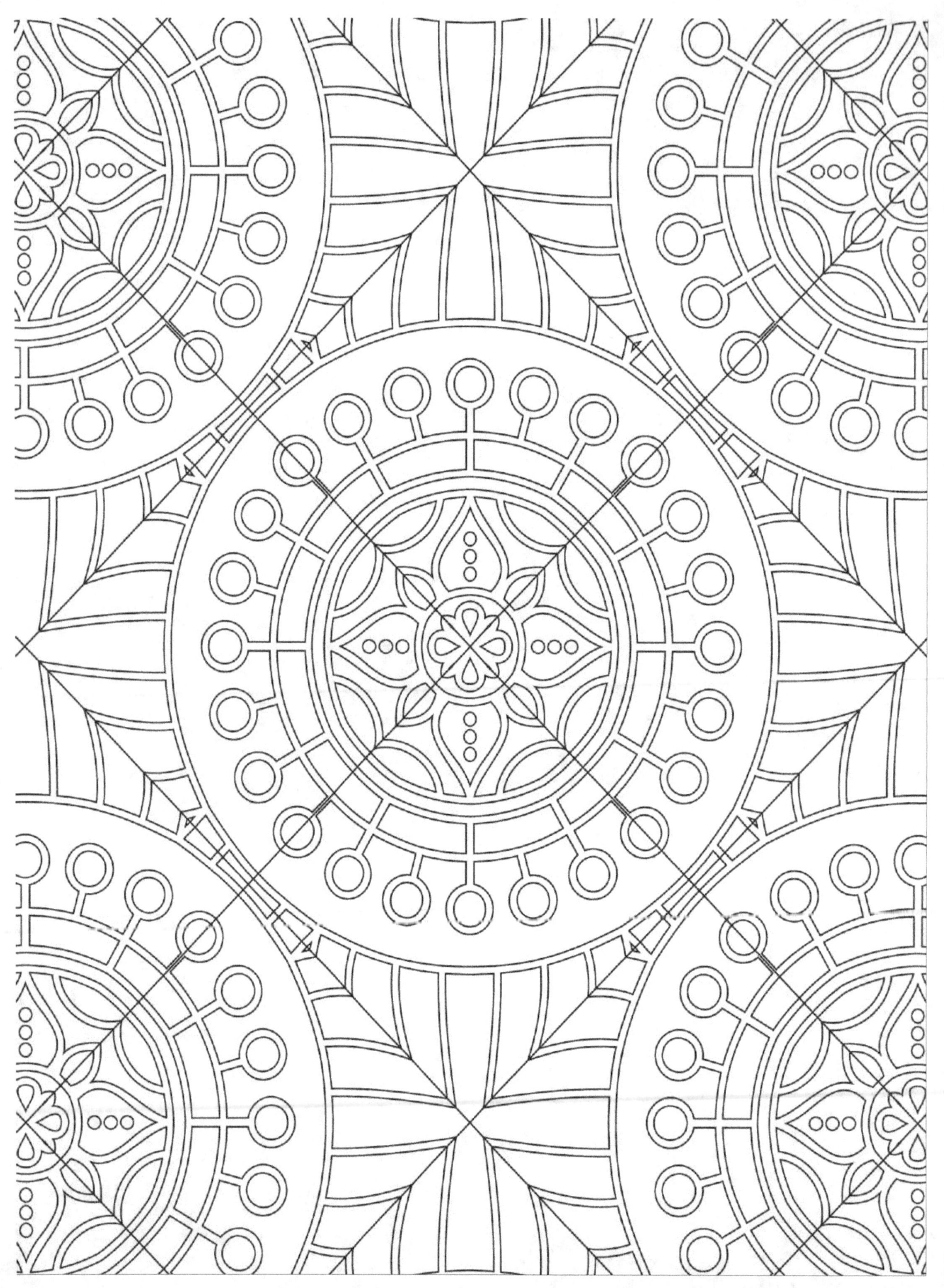

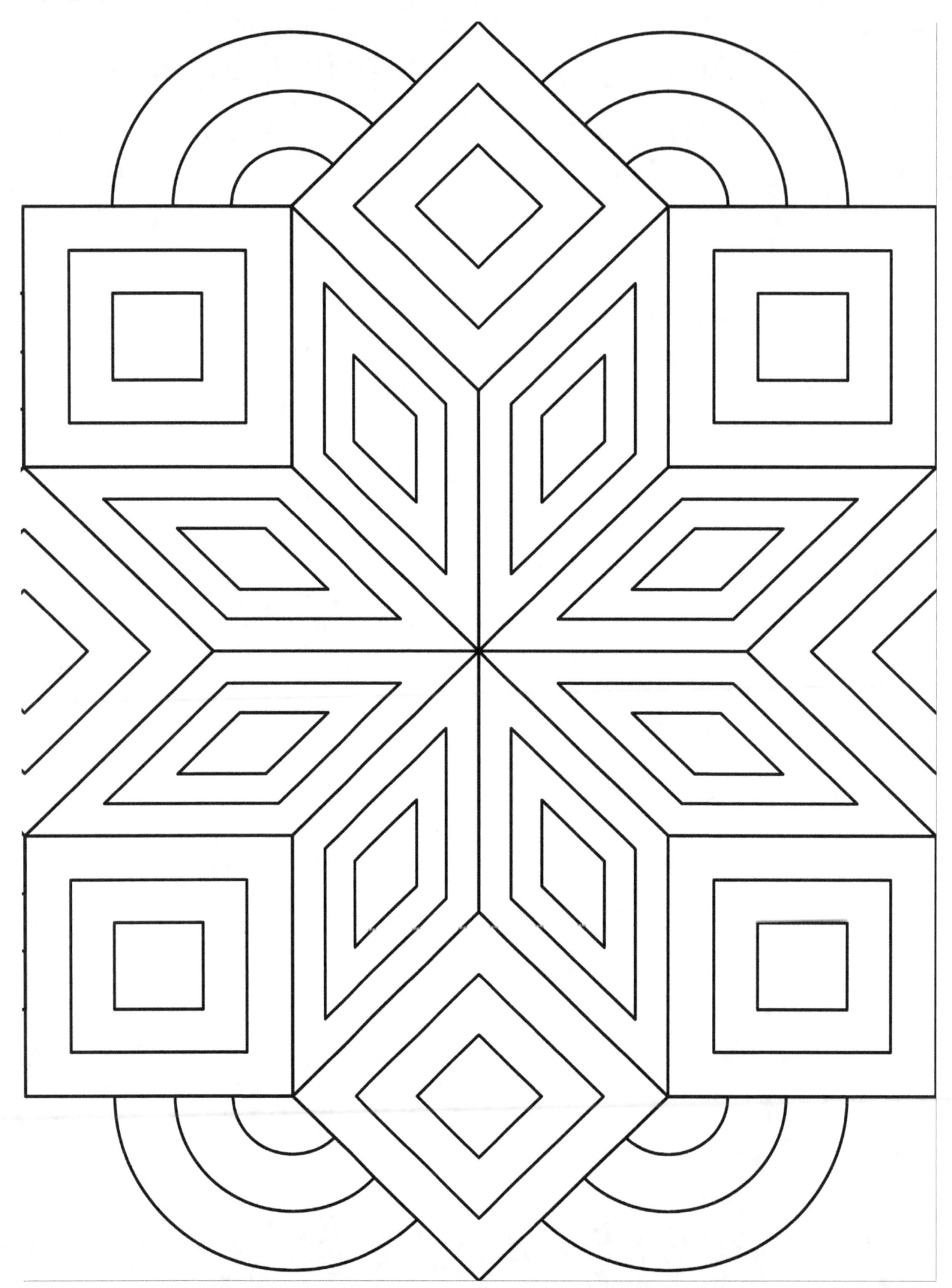

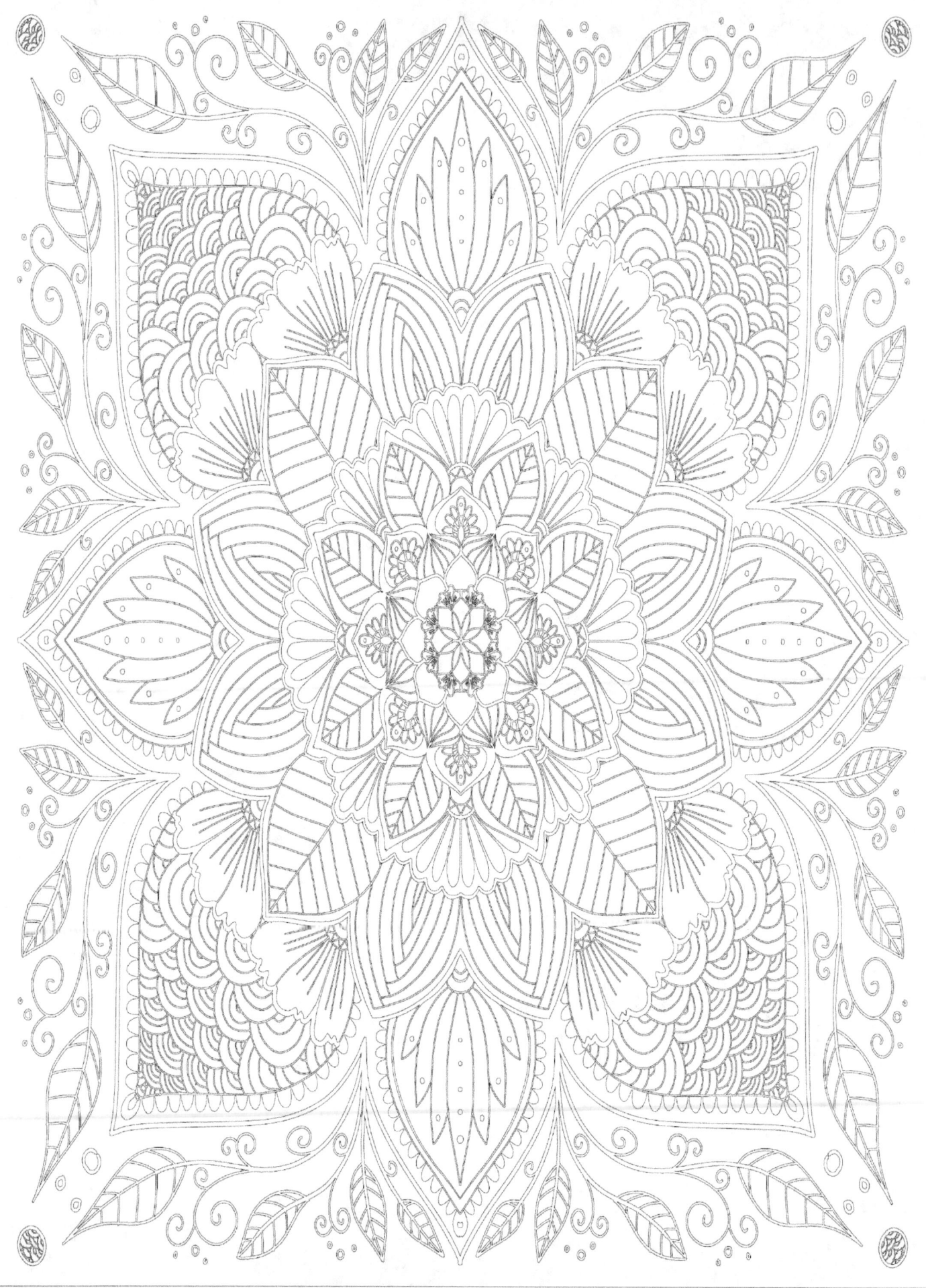

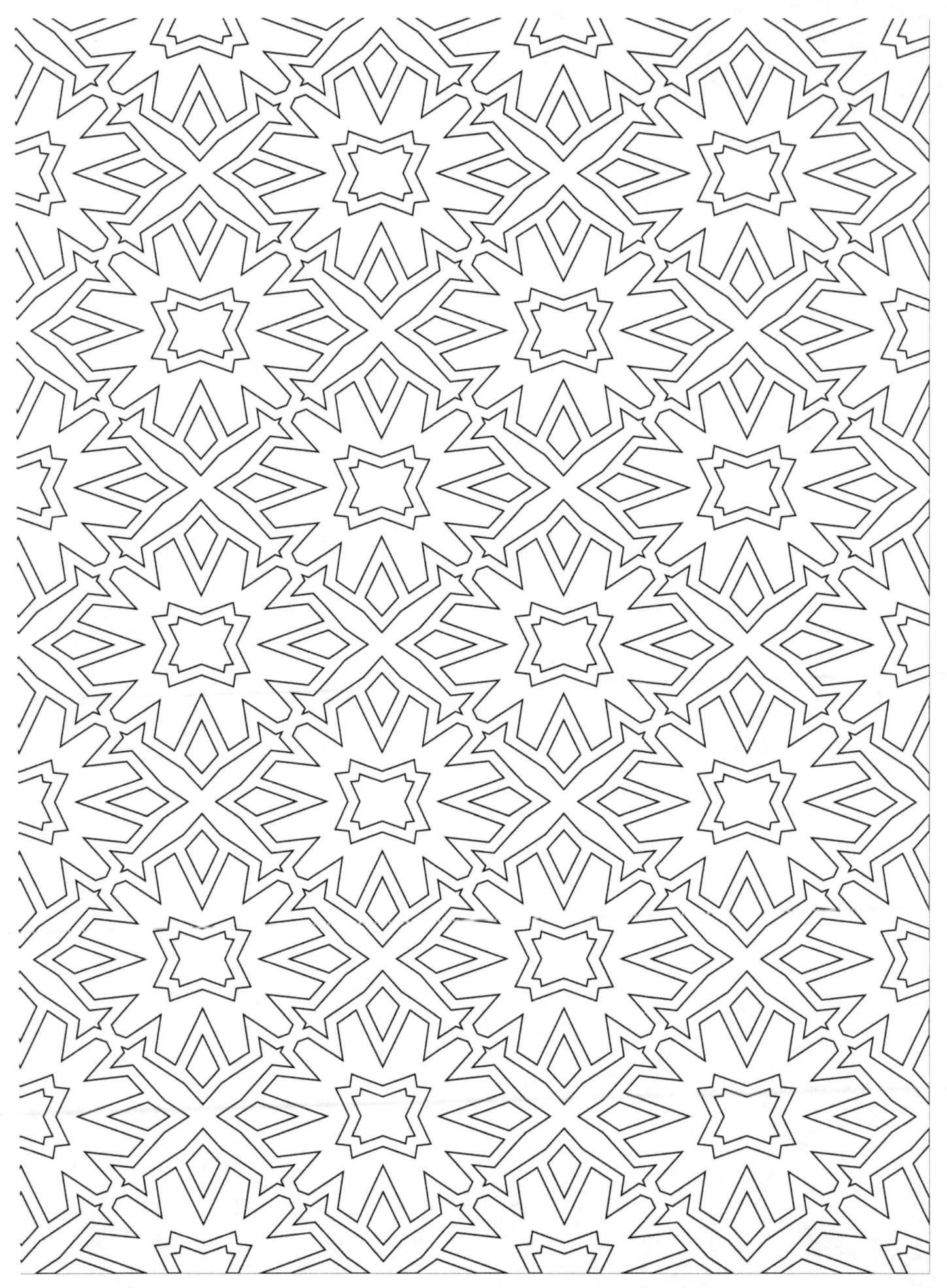

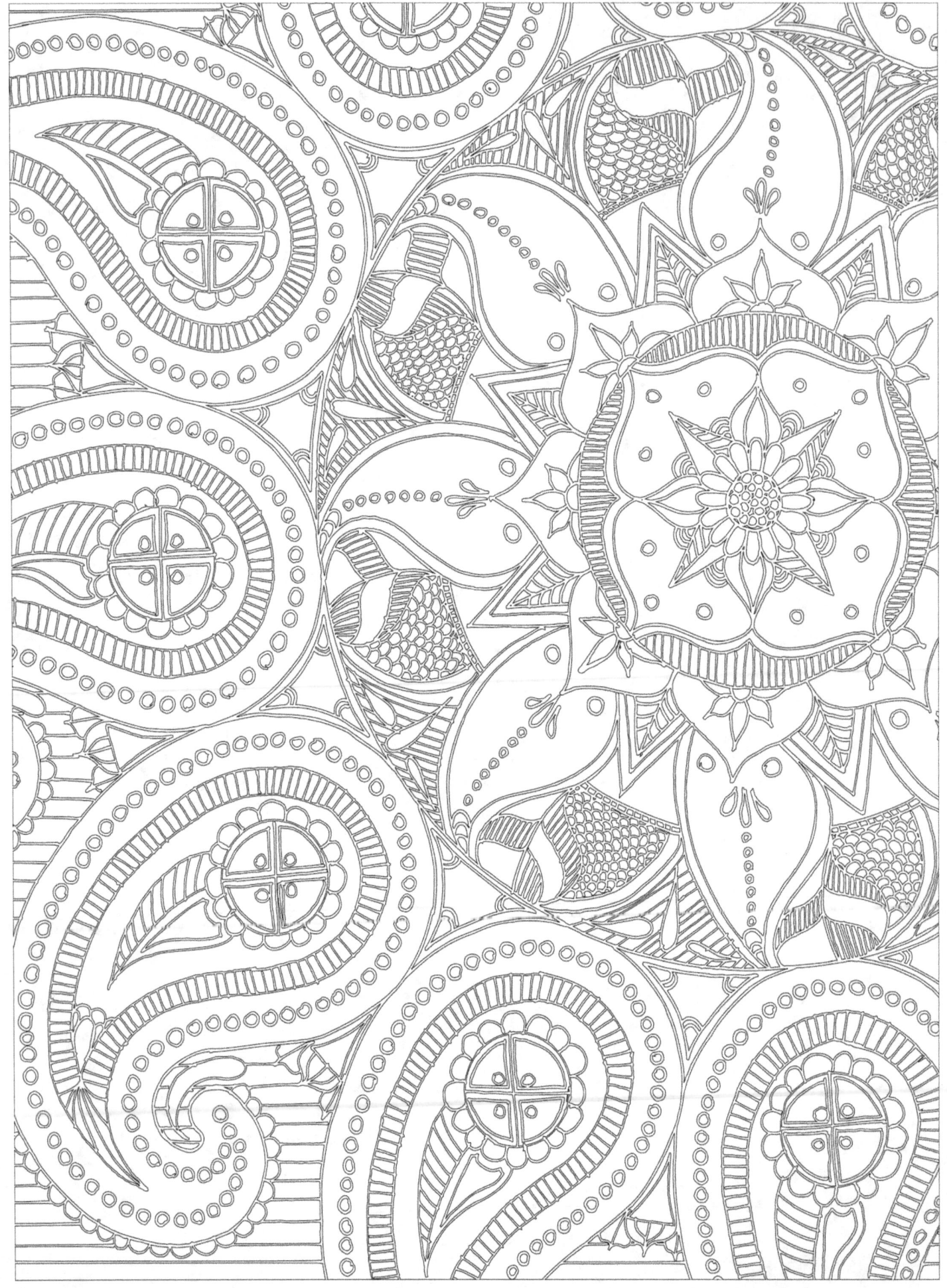

www.ingramcontent.com/pod-product-compliance
Lightning Source LLC
Chambersburg PA
CBHW080844220526
45467CB00008B/2381